BAPTISM

WHAT WAY IS THE RIGHT WAY?

APOSTLE TERRY W. ROGERS

Baptism – What Way Is the Right Way?

© 2019 Apostle Terry W. Rogers

Printed in the USA

ISBN (Print Version): 978-1097524181

All Rights Reserved. This book is protected by the copyright laws of the United States of America. This book may not be copied or reprinted for commercial gain or profit. The use of short quotations is permitted. Permission will be granted upon request. The author guarantees all contents are original and do not infringe upon the legal rights of any other person or work.

Cover design: GermanCreative
Publisher: Shekinah Glory Publishing

www.shekinahglorypublishing.org

ACKNOWLEDGMENTS

I would like to thank God for answering my prayer and enabling me to write books for people who want to know the truth of God's Word.

For those who worship God, must worship Him in Spirit and in Truth.

To my Pastor, the late Dr. D. Rayford Bell, former Presiding Bishop of the P.C.A.F. Organization; thanks for teaching me holiness and the Apostle's Doctrine, thank God for someone who loved the Lord!

To my family thanks for your support and your patience.

To my son Elijah; teach the Word in season and out of season, be faithful, and teach no other Doctrine.

Thanks to Evangelist Candy Johnson for her assistance and encouragement during the editing process of this book.

Thanks, Marilyn Benton, for supporting my family through difficult times.

Thanks for your support, Stephen Scruggs.

Thanks, Grandma Flora Peterson for everything.

Thanks, Mary Ellen Willis for encouraging me to go to Bible College.

To all the saints at Christ Temple thank you for your support.

Redeem Team Home of the Street Preachers

TABLE OF CONTENTS

Introduction	9
Chapter One What Is the Definition Of Baptism?	13
Chapter Two The Symbolism of Baptism	23
Chapter Three The Power of the Water	27
Chapter Four Repentance	33
Chapter Five New Testament Baptism	39
Chapter Six The History of Baptism	53
Chapter Seven The Baptism of the Spirit	63
Chapter Eight The Aftermath	87
Chapter Nine The Baptism of Suffering	95
Chapter Ten The Master Trick of the Devil	101
Chapter Eleven The Blood Test	109
Chapter Twelve The Eyes of Discernment	113
Summary	117
Baptized Into the Body Hymn	119
Altar Call	121

Baptismal Formula	123
The Water Way Hymn	125
Certificate of Baptism	127
Great Cloud Of Baptismal	129
About the Author	131
Bibliography	133
Study Bibles	134
Other Publications	135
Support/Contact Information	137

EPHESIANS 4:5
ONE LORD, ONE FAITH, ONE BAPTISM

INTRODUCTION

This book is designed to give you information on baptism and provide knowledge on this subject and to help others come into the knowledge of the scriptural way of baptism. Solving the question of who is right, and who is wrong, scripturally by applying the Word of God only.

In modern times, we have many denominations, religious false prophets, and anti-Christ. These people lack understanding and have twisted scriptural meanings to their own advantage. Beware of false prophets, which come to you in sheep's clothing, but inwardly they are ravening wolves [Matthew 7:21]. People having a nature as a sheep "are easily led astray like sheep without a shepherd." Many have been taught part of the gospel and have commandments of men and doctrines of men and devils, so we must study to show ourselves approved unto God. Some of God's people will be destroyed because of a lack of knowledge. Nothing but the righteous will see God. It is my goal and the Redeem Team Home of the Street Preachers, to see that you know the Truth, for the truth, shall set you free!

The knowledge of the Scriptures is very important to Christians everywhere. It is our defense, against the devil, his lies, man traditions, and false prophets to preserve the knowledge of the Scriptures. There are many churches that are applying the wrong formula when baptizing people. They are baptizing according to tradition, but tradition will make the Word of God of none effect. The devil capitalizes on these errors by performing false signs and lying wonders. He also masquerades pseudo-healing to keep people bound in error. Be mindful, that whatever God does it is perfect. You can't add to it, or take away from it, ninety-nine and a half won't do.

It must be 100% Word. It must be Scripture upon Scripture, line upon line, and precept upon precept, **by every Word of God.**

There is a remarkable blessing that accompanies the baptismal ceremony. Amazingly, as one passes through the waters of judgment safely, of dying and rising with Christ, and having their sins remitted and washed away, there are significant truths and eternal validation, which ought to be applicable for such an occasion, by giving God the glory and the praise.

NEVER STOP LEARNING

Apollo's a preaching machine, a great preacher of Alexandria, came to Ephesus. He was eloquent and mighty in Scriptures. Somehow, he knew only the baptism of John the Baptist, the baptism of repentance [Acts 19:4]. The baptism he was acquainted with was not sufficient for salvation. Priscilla and Aquilla, a first-century missionary husband and wife team of the Gospel, showed him a more excellent way, [1Corinthians 12:31] found in the Apostle's Doctrine of baptism. In this, you will find the Doctrine of the Name of Jesus Christ who is the Great Apostle of our Faith. This informs us that as disciples, we are teachable and able to learn more from the Word of God in the spirit of meekness. It is the Word of God that empowers, enlighten, enables, and equips us to a more perfect way of performing things spiritually.

In both the spiritual and natural realms, we can learn something daily. As we search the Scripture, it requires an open mind, an open heart, and an open Bible. An open Bible will unleash and teach a closed heart and mind to receive the things of God [1 Corinthian 2:14]. Today can be your out-date and road to recovery. Lean not to your own understanding which consists of disappointments and set-backs, but have faith in God (Mark 11:22), and believe in Jesus (Acts 16:31). Acknowledge the Lord in all thy ways, He will direct thy paths. (Proverbs 3:5, 6)

CHAPTER ONE

What Is Baptism?

Jesus answered, "Verily, verily, I say unto thee, except a man be born of <u>water and of the Spirit</u>, he cannot enter into the kingdom of God." [John 3:5]

In the time in which we live many people have been baptized by their family church without any knowledge of what they are doing and why they are doing it.

Baptism plays a major role in being saved according to the Scriptures in [John 3:5]. It states that you must be born of the water and of the Spirit. Therefore, being born of the water and of the Spirit is very important, as well as having the name of Jesus pronounced over you, as you are immersed in water. The name of Jesus means the authority of Jesus. The key to performing this deed is obedience to the Word of God, by submission to that name [Col. 3:17; James 4:7]. Also keep in mind that the Father, the Word, and The HOLY GHOST are one [1 John 5:7]. So, to be born again of the Spirit means to be born again according to the Will of God, according to the Word of God and according to the Spirit of God [John 1:13]. You are authorized to be born again like the Father, Word, and Holy Ghost command.

Flesh, blood and the will of man cannot inherit the Kingdom of God [1 Cor. 15:50]. Being born of the will of God, we have an inheritance that is incorruptible, and undefiled, and that fadeth not away, reserved in heaven for you [1 Pet. 1:4].

The baptisms of ancient times are a shadow of the baptisms to come in the New Testament [Exodus 30:18-21]. God told Moses to make a laver of brass for the priest to wash with water that they shouldn't die.

During these ancient times, all the priests were to wash at the laver before the Presence of the Lord before any ministry or function may be performed. He is telling us that there must be holiness or separation from all defilements of the flesh as we enter his Presence.

Washing before prayer or sacrifice was a custom and considered notable among all ancient nations. Washing was a sign of spiritual purity and a sense of physical cleanness. The proselytes were baptized and washed as a part of initiatory rites to the community. This practice was performed in the community where the Dead Sea Scrolls were found. Peter stated we are "A Royal Priesthood" [1 Peter 2:9], therefore we must be washed.

Just looking at the water does not make anyone clean. The sprinkling of water does not make anyone clean. Being baptized in the Father, Son, and Holy Ghost does not make anyone clean. The Word mentions being baptized in the name of the Father, Son, and Holy Ghost. [Matthew 28:19] What is the name? And she shall bring forth a Son, and thou shalt call His name Jesus [Matthew 1:21]. Once you are completely immersed in the water [John 3:5] and the name of Jesus pronounced over your life, the effects in that name immediately go to work in your life. The NAME (JESUS), rather than titles (FATHER, SON, and HOLY GHOST) means the authority of Jesus. Then ought the name, rather than titles, be called over an individual doing baptism? Jesus said I come in my Father's name [John 5:43]. Note there is only one name called over an individual in comparison to three titles.

There is none other name under heaven given among men whereby, we must be saved [Acts 4:12]. The water (being baptized) as well as the name Jesus must be applied. It is the application of the name Jesus which cleanses and remits one of their sins. This truth must be applied personally to the life of every individual in order for its cleansing power to be effective in their lives.

The divers washing under the law gives proof in the New Testament [John 2:6]. There were six water pots for the purification of the Jews. The number of man is six. It was on the sixth day God created man. The baptism ceremony is performed as one takes on the identification of the death, burial, and resurrection of our Lord and Savior Christ Jesus. Its initiatory rite of being born again of the water is by applying faith in the Lord Jesus Christ [John 3:1-21].

As we look at the meaning of baptism it comes from the Greek word "baptisma" which means consisting of the process of submersion in water. *Bapto,* means to dip. The Scripture is positively clear that baptism is immersion in water. [Rom 6:4; Col. 2:14]. Water is a type of both the Spirit and the Word, as stated in [John 7: 37-39; Eph 5:26].

Many people throughout the world who fight baptism will say, water does not save. Well, it does according to the Scripture [John 3:5; 1 Peter 3:18-22], "even baptism doth also now save us", but I also understand you can be baptized and still come up without a penitent heart. Therefore, we must be mindful and remember a baby does not come into the world walking, he crawls first. Every individual must go through the process. Take off your spiritual boxing gloves and go through the process of being born again properly in Jesus' name.

Baptism is also an ordinance, statue or degree given to the church, by Jesus Christ that must be obeyed. To the Jewish sect of Judaism, to baptize by the authority of the Lord Jesus Christ meant giving up all fellowship with his nation, Judaism, and all political rights and privileges. Today, the family of Jewish people would disown any family member who acknowledges Jesus Christ as Lord and Savior. They would go as far as cutting off all inheritance and having a funeral for that individual. It was serious and it's all because Jesus is considered amongst them as a Prophet and not the Son of God. Jesus was deliberately disdained and rejected by his own (John 1:11).

As Jesus Christ was approaching thirty years of age, he began His ministry [Luke 3:21, 23]. As the High Priest and His sons were washed [Ex 29:4, Num. 4:3], Christ came as High Priest, and his ministry was inaugurated in a traditional manner by washing with water [Matthew 3:13]. Are we greater than Jesus Christ? The answer is No! Therefore, we need to be baptized in water according to Holy Scripture. Jesus never broke the Scripture nor took away from the Scripture [Deut. 4:2]. He came to fulfill the Scripture [Matt. 5:17].

There Are Several Baptisms

1. The Earth being baptized in water 40 days and 40 nights [Gen 7:12].
2. Eight souls were saved by water [1 Peter 3:21].
3. And were all baptized unto Moses in the cloud and in the sea; [1Cor. 10:2]
4. Water Baptism to repentance [John's baptism Matt 3:11].

5. New Testament Water Baptism [Acts 2:38, 8:16, 10:45-48, 19:1-6]
6. Spirit Baptism [Acts 2:1-4, Acts 1:8, Acts 43-48, 19:6]
7. Baptism of Sufferings [Mark 10:38; Luke 12:20]
8. The Baptism of Death [Heb. 9:27; Rom. 6:3]

We are commissioned to "Go ye therefore, and teach all nations, baptizing them in the name of the Father, and of the Son, and of the Holy Ghost: [Matt. 28:19]." The Father, Son, and Holy Ghost are "Titles" and are not a name. If a father gives his son a check and puts "Son" on it, the son will not be able to cash it because there is no name on it. Therefore, the check is void, ineffective and inoperative.

[Acts 2:38] Then Peter said to them, "Repent, and let every one of you be baptized in the name of Jesus Christ for the remission of sins; and you shall receive the gift of the Holy Spirit."

[Acts 8:12] But when they believed Philip as he preached the things concerning the kingdom of God and the name of Jesus Christ, both men and women were baptized.

[Acts 8:35-38] And the eunuch said, "See, here is water. What hinders me from being baptized?" Then Philip said, "If you believe with all your heart you may." And he answered and said, "I believe that Jesus Christ is the Son of God." …. both Philip and the Eunuch went down into the water, and he baptized him.

Water baptism, the baptism of John the Baptist, is the outward symbol and declaration that one desires to serve God and do HIS will to the best of their ability. There is a difference between the water baptism of John the Baptist and the water baptism implemented by the Apostles in the book of Acts.

The baptism in Jesus' name was instructed by Jesus but performed by the apostles [John 4:1-2; Matthew 28:19]. The two baptisms are similar in many ways, but their differences are quite striking. Both baptized in water and both constitute confession and repentance.

The variations are that John baptism does not wash away sin nor remit one of their sins [Acts 19:4]. The baptism in Jesus' name washes away and forgives us of our sin [Acts 2:38]. Without the shedding of blood, there is no remission [Hebrew 9:22].

John's baptism is mentioned in the Gospel and the book of Acts. Paul elaborated on the prophecy of John the Baptist; It is He, who coming after me, is preferred before me [John 1:27]. After the disciples of John heard Paul preaching, they were baptized again [Acts 19:1-5].

And I (Paul) went up by revelation and communicated unto them (Aquila and Priscilla) that gospel which I preach among the Gentiles, but privately to them which were of reputation [Galatians 2:2]. This technique Aquila and Priscilla learned from Apostle Paul teaching in private thereafter, they applied this method to Apollos.

[24] And a certain Jew named Apollos, born at Alexandria, an eloquent man, and mighty in the scriptures came to Ephesus.
[25] This man was instructed in *the way of the Lord*; and being fervent in the spirit, he spake and taught diligently *the things of the Lord*, knowing only the baptism of John.
[26] And he began to speak boldly in the synagogue: whom when Aquila and Priscilla had heard, they took him unto them and expounded unto him *the way of God* more perfectly. [Acts 18:24-28]. What is the way of God? Jesus is the Way. No one comes to the Father except through me [John 14:6]. By the way, my name is Jesus.

The baptism in Jesus' name is mentioned frequently throughout the New Testament.

Seven- The Perfect Number of God

Note: There is no record of infant baptism in the bible by Jesus Christ or none of his apostles or John the Baptist.

This practice is a non-biblical practice by the Catholic Church performed during the 2nd century but became general in the 6th century. We should be careful not to add to the Word of God and not to take away from the Word of God.

There is no record of sprinkling water as a baptism in the New Testament, this came from men who started their own religion. [Romans 1:25] says, "**Who changed the truth of God into a lie** and worshipped and served the creature more than the Creator, who is blessed forever.

[2 Thessalonians 2:11-12] says, "And for this cause, <u>God shall send a strong delusion,</u> *that they should believe a lie*: **That they all might be damned who believe not the truth** but had pleasure in unrighteousness.

[Rev 22:18-19] says, "For I testify unto you every man that heareth the words of the prophecy of this book, **if any man shall add unto these things**, God shall add unto him the plagues that are written in this book (The Holy Bible). And if any man shall take away from the words of this book (The Holy Bible) of this prophecy, God shall take away his part out of the holy city, and from the things which are written in this book (The Holy Bible).

As the Heart Pants After The Water Brook

*[**Psalms 42:1**] (KJV)* [1] *As the hart panteth after the water brooks, so panteth my soul after thee, O God.*

The first 10 psalms of Korah are called the Psalms for backsliding Jews. They are Psalms for when King David was in exile and destined to return to Jerusalem. He was haunted and chased down by his enemies, for his life. Them that opposed him mocked him by saying, "Where is your God now."

[Psalms 42:2] <u>*My soul thirsteth for God*</u>*, for the living God: when shall I come and appear before God?*

This psalm paints a picture of a young hart (doe) being chased, and they are making a comparison between David and the young hart. When a hart is haunted, he will flee to the river or the water brook. There the hart will submerge himself as to hide or cover himself, in fear of the hunters, and the dogs chasing him. He then flows downstream by swimming and submerging himself, while alluding his hunters by way of water.

[Psalms 42:7]   Deep calleth unto deep at the noise of thy waterspouts: all thy waves and <u>thy billows are gone over me</u>.

As he submerges into the water brook, it throws off the hart scent to confuse and ensure that the dogs are unable to find him. You must be in a place with God where the enemy is unable to find you. That place is known as the secret place [Psalms 91:1]. Be mindful that the dogs in the Scriptures are the **false prophets**. They are the hellhounds barking, but God says they can bark and make up a lot of noise, but they can't bite you. Daniel was in the den with the lions, but they couldn't devour him because he was in that secret place (prayer).

Psalm 42

TO THE CHIEF MUSICIAN, MASCHIL, FOR THE SONS OF KORAH.

1. As the hart panteth after the water brooks, so panteth my soul after thee, O God.
2. My soul thirsteth for God, for the living God: when shall I come and appear before God?
3. My tears have been my meat day and night, while they continually say unto me, Where is thy God?
4. When I remember these things, I pour out my soul in me: for I had gone with the multitude, I went with them to the house of God, with the voice of joy and praise, with a multitude that kept holy day.
5. Why art thou cast down, O my soul? and why art thou disquieted in me? hope thou in God: for I shall yet praise him for the help of his countenance.
6. O my God, my soul is cast down within me: therefore, will I remember thee from the land of Jordan, and of the Hermonites, from the hill Mizar.
7. Deep calleth unto deep at the noise of thy waterspouts: all thy waves and thy billows are gone over me.
8. Yet the LORD will command his lovingkindness in the daytime, and in the night his song shall be with me, and my prayer unto the God of my life.
9. I will say unto God my rock, Why hast thou forgotten me? why go I mourning because of the oppression of the enemy?
10. As with a sword in my bones, mine enemies reproach me; while they say daily unto me, Where is thy God?
11. Why art thou cast down, O my soul? and why art thou disquieted within me? hope thou in God: for I shall yet praise him, who is the health of my countenance, and my God.

CHAPTER TWO

The Symbolism of Baptism

Know ye not, that so many of us as <u>were baptized into Jesus Christ</u> were baptized into his death? [Romans 6:3]

The Bible, as we know is very symbolic in its parables of dark sayings that illuminate great light on the knowledge that was kept secret before the foundations of the world; and now is revealed onto us by His holy Apostles and Prophets.

Symbolism is an object that has a representation of something else. It is figurative in meaning.

<u>**The symbolic meaning of baptism had many representations.**</u>
The first one was an outward sign of repentance according to John the Baptist. Thousands of people came from near and far to be transformed from the corrupt person they were. They came acknowledging their sin with the desire to be saved from their sin and shame.

<u>**But John's baptism was only to prepare them to receive total forgiveness for sins, and to baptize them into Jesus Christ and with fire**</u> [Matt 3:11; Acts 19:1-6]. In the book of Acts, the Apostle Paul re-baptized the converts of John the Baptist into the name of Jesus Christ and the disciples spoke in tongues as the Spirit gave utterance. **Those who were saved under the Law were saved under the instructions from God for that time**. But when Jesus was crucified and rose from the dead, everyone fell under a new and living way of doing things, due to the dispensation of grace. For the

law was given by Moses (the dispensation of the law), but grace and truth (the dispensation of grace) came by Jesus Christ. [John 1:17]

Baptism was a symbol of purity that literally means to wash or to be regenerated [Titus 3:5; Eph 5:26].

<u>**Another symbolic meaning "is a new beginning"**</u> according to the book of Genesis in the story of Noah. The whole Earth was fully immersed in the water for forty days and nights [Gen 7:12, Gen 8:1-3]. The Earth had a new start with Noah and his sons [1Pet 3:18-22]. The number 40 means probationary, testing, closing in victory or judgment.

The leper Naaman represents deliverance and healing in the body and the spirit [2 Kings 5:14]. The story begins with the prophet Elisha telling Naaman to go and dip himself in the River Jordan seven times which represents God's perfect number. This was a hard pill to swallow, very difficult to decide. He wanted to do it his way. Many of us want to perform the baptismal our way. There are many Christians who are not willing to be re-baptized according to the Scriptures. But here is a man instructed to dip more than once or twice. He was to dip ***seven times*** in dirty water. His healing and deliverance came from his willingness to obey God. The Prophets of Old represented God Himself. The foundation of the Bible rests upon the holy Apostles and the Prophets. (Read 2 Kings 5:13).

When Jesus Christ met John the Baptist to be baptized in the River Jordan [Matt 3:13-17]; baptism had another symbolic meaning. "It meant to fulfill all righteousness" and we learn that it was a sign that a person was or wanted to be righteous [Matt 5: 10; 1 Peter 4:18]. **<u>Christ who had no sin received baptism out of obedience of His own Word and submission to the Father</u>** [John 1:1; Heb. 5:8-10; Matt 5:17-18]. It was Jesus (Word) that fulfilled all righteousness.

Ought we to obey His Word? Your answer - Whereby, Jesus having submitted to the Father by obedience, we to must submit to God and resist the Devil and yield to the Spirit of God. [James 4:7]

The next symbolic meaning is the burial of the old man and the beginning of the new man in Christ Jesus our Lord. It also represents for the Christian to be buried with Jesus through immersion into the water thus being identified with Christ, according to [Romans 6:4-5; Colossians 2: 12] this, also symbolizes his death.

After someone dies, the burial takes place. If the person is not dead, he is alive, and we do not want to bury a man alive. We do not want anyone covered with mud, but we want everyone covered with the blood. Therefore, Jesus was dead when they put him in the tomb. The believer must be repentant and dead to sin, self, and the world. [1 Corinthians 15: 22].

History tells of some people who died and was not baptized the proper way according to the Scriptures. Their friends and relatives wanted to baptize them, for they knew what the apostles said according to [Acts 2:38].

The Marcionites and the Gnostics baptized the dead, but it was too late [1Corinthians 15:22]! There is no wisdom nor salvation beyond the grave.

[Psalms 115: 17] says, "The dead praise not the Lord, neither any that go down, into silence."

[Ecclesiastes 8:8] says, "There is no man that hath power over the spirit to retain the spirit; neither hath he powers in the day of death: and there is no discharge in that war; neither shall wickedness deliver those that are given to it."

[Hebrews 9:27] says, "And as it is appointed unto men once to die, but after death the judgment."

Baptism is also symbolic of the blood atonement of Jesus Christ. The symbolic meaning is to be washed with the sinless blood of Jesus Christ, the sacrificial Lamb of God. The theory is if a Christian had not been washed in the name of Jesus he had not been washed in the blood of the Lamb.

In Greek, the cult Mithraism was one of the major religions of the Roman Empire. Mithra was the god of light and wisdom and its members were to slay a bull and be washed in its blood as a symbol of being born again.

Finally, it represents the Spirit of baptism in the book of [Ephesians 4:5] which states, "One Lord, One Faith, One Baptism." [Acts 2:1-4, 2:38, 8:16, 10:44-47, 19:1-6]. We must be married to Christ, taking upon ourselves His name and His power! But some people want to shack up with Jesus and are not willing to marry Him for better or for worse until death do you part.

[Acts 1:8] says, "But ye shall receive power, after that the Holy Ghost is come upon you: and ye shall be witnesses unto me both in Jerusalem, and in all Judaea, and in Samaria, and unto the uttermost part of the Earth."

CHAPTER THREE

The Power of The Water

Does Water Really Save People?

Which sometime were disobedient, when once the long-suffering of God waited in the days of Noah, while the ark was a preparing, wherein few, that is, <u>eight souls were saved by water!</u> The like figure whereunto even baptism <u>doth also save us</u> (not the putting away of the filth of the flesh, but the answer of a good conscience toward God), by the resurrection of Jesus Christ.
[1 Peter 3:21- 22]

In the beginning, there was water [Genesis 1:2; Psalms 148:4]. The spirit of God moved on the face of the waters. Even the earth was covered with water in the beginning and God called the dry land forth and called it Earth [Genesis 1:9-10]. This was the same substance that God used to create Man. He made himself a mud man and blew the breath of life (Spirit) into him and man became a living soul [Genesis 2:7].

[1 John 5:8] says, "And there are three that bear witness in earth, the Spirit (God), and the water (Word), and the blood (life is in the Blood): and these three agree in one."

<u>Science teaches that man's body contains all the elements that are found in the earth</u>. This brings to mind at funerals "ashes, to ashes, dust to dust." The earth and man have a lot in common. The earth is surrounded by nearly three-fourths water, and the body is about eighty percent water. The body needs water to survive and to be cleansed. The body without water (the WORD) will cause the body to dehydrate and die. Our souls without the Word will die. Jesus is the Resurrection and the Life; He resurrects things that have died or

things that are dying. Open the door and let Him in.

The Lord Jesus Christ came by water (Word) and the blood (Spirit), even Jesus Christ; not by water only, but by water and the blood. And it is the Spirit that beareth witness because the Spirit is Truth [1 John 5:6]. On the cross, at Calvary, something happened that was amazing. One of the soldiers took a spear and pierced Jesus' side and blood and water came out.

[John 19:34] says, "But one of the soldiers with a spear pierced his side, and forthwith came there out blood and water. **(Spirit, which is the blood and the Truth, which is the Word (Living Water).**

Understanding the natural makes it possible for you to understand the spiritual. The earth is used as an object to mankind in the story of Noah [Genesis 6:5-8]. The earth was filled with wickedness and every imagination of the thoughts of man's heart was evil continually. So, God decided to destroy all things that did not repent. **He chose to immerge the whole earth in water by raining on the earth forty days and forty nights until the earth (man's body) was completely underwater, just like baptism.**

Afterward, we find a new environment. A place where only holy people and all the animals of God creation dwell with them. Another paradise! A new beginning [1 Peter 3:18-22]

The Apostle Paul said, "That all things would become new if you were in Christ [2 Corinthians 5:17]. The key to this Scripture is being in Christ.

The power of the water is a fact in Scripture, as we look at the prophet Moses, we find that he also experiences a baptism by water. [1 Corinthians 10:1-6]

[1 Corinthians 10:2] says, "**And were all baptized unto Moses in the cloud and in the sea.** The cloud represented the Spirit, and the Red Sea represented the water (Word)."

[1 Corinthians 10:3] says, "And did eat the **same spiritual meat (Word, Bible, are the same interpretation).**"

[1 Corinthians 10:4] says, "**And did all drink the same spiritual drink:** for they drank of that spiritual Rock that followed them: and that Rock was Christ."

When Moses and the people of Israel came out of Egypt, they were saved by water from Pharaoh, and his army was drowned in the sea [Exodus 14:29-31; 15:8-11]. The nation of Israel was baptized through the Red Sea. It was only one way for the Old Testament believers to be saved. The scripture says, "He that believeth is baptized and he that believeth not shall be dammed [Mark 16: 16]."

There was another figure of baptism in the Old Testament. It is the passage of the Jordan River. The young warrior Joshua leads the people of Israel into the promised land through the River Jordan, in like manner as Moses led the Israelites through the Red Sea. The next generation had to be baptized and each proceeding generation. To be baptized is a prerequisite to salvation. It is a requirement.

[Joshua 3:13] says, "And it shall come to pass, as soon as the soles of your feet of the priest that bear the ark of the Lord, the Lord of all the earth, shall rest in the waters of Jordan shall be cut off from the waters that come down from above; and they shall stand upon a heap."

This was a type of death with Jesus Christ [Romans 6:6-11; Ephesians 2:5-6; Colossians 3:1-3]. The prophet Elisha is used to bringing forth the next figure of the water as its cure's Naaman from leprosy. **He was asked to dip seven times in the Jordan River** [2 Kings 5:13-15] and was healed by his own obedience. This is what it's all about, repentance and obedience [1 Samuel15: 22].

The baptism of Jesus Christ [Mark 1:9-11; Luke 3:21-22; John 1: 31-34; Matthew 3:13-17] shows us that Jesus knew the power of the water and was baptized by John the Baptist who baptized with water unto repentance. Jesus who needed not to repent, **or neither was He**

born in sin, was baptized to fulfill all righteousness.

[Matthew 3:15] says, "And Jesus answering said unto him, suffer it to be so now: for thus it becometh us to fulfill all righteousness. Then he suffered him."

The New Testament Baptism in water by the Apostles of Jesus Christ invokes the name of Jesus only [Acts 2:38, 8:16, 36, 10, 48; 19:5-6]; all these scriptures explain [Matt 28:19]. In the New Testament, it was necessary to be baptized in the water. To be saved there are many religions that are trying to omit the baptism of water. This practice is illegal against Scripture. Even if you have received the Spirit baptism, you are still required by Scripture to obey or fulfill all righteousness as Jesus. The Apostle Peter witness the Gentiles receiving the Holy Ghost before they were baptized. But the Apostle knew the importance of being baptized with water, and that it was a commandment.

[Acts 10:47] says, "Can any man forbid water? That these should not be baptized, which have received the Holy Ghost as well as we."

[Acts 10:48] says, "And he commanded them to be baptized in the name of the Lord (Jesus is the Lord). Then prayed him to tarry certain days."

Many believe that water does not save an individual, but the Scriptures say it does [1 Peter 3:20; John 3:5; Mark 16:16]. Never argue with Scripture, because you won't win! Just believe the Scripture as it is written. Scripture is written to always be agreed with, never disagree or debate with Scripture.

[Mark 16:16] says, "He that believeth and is baptized shall be saved, but he that believeth not shall be damned."

Remember the Samaritan woman at the well [John 4:1-42]. Jesus said unto her, "Whosoever drinketh of this water shall never thirst again!" She was given the choice to be a partaker of things eternal. It was up to her to make a choice to receive it or reject it. It is up to you to make that same decision. To receive it is to acknowledge it, to reject it is to be discarded.

[John 7:37-38] says, "In the last day, that great day of the feast, Jesus stood and cried, saying, if any man thirst, let him come unto Me, and drink. He that believeth on me (Jesus Christ), as the Scriptures (The Holy Bible) hath said, out of his belly shall flow rivers of living water."

Above all the individual must do his part, when it comes to water baptism. The Lord will do his part by remitting your sins. If you do not repent, coupled with faith, you will not get the full effect. Remember, it is through obedience that you get total results, or you will go down a dry devil and get up a wet devil [Romans 1:5; Acts 15:8-9].

[Acts 15:8-9] says, "And God which knoweth the hearts bare them, witness, giving them the Holy Ghost, even as he did unto us. And put no difference between us (the Apostles and the Jews) and them (Cornelius and his house) **purifying their hearts by faith."**

CHAPTER FOUR

Repentance

Bring forth, therefore, fruits meet for repentance.
[Matthew 3:8]

The constituent of repentance has been preached by the Old and New Testament Prophets. [Deuteronomy 30:10; 2 Kings 17:13; Jeremiah 8:6; Ezekiel 14:6, 18:30].

[Deuteronomy 30:10] says, "If thou shalt hearken unto the voice of the Lord thy God, to keep his commandments and his statutes which are written in his book of the law, and if thou turn unto the Lord thy God with all thine heart, and with all thy soul."

[Hebrews 1:1] says, "God who at sundry times and in divers' manners spake in time past unto the fathers by the Prophets."

[Hebrews 1:2] says, "Hath in these last days spoken unto us by his Son, by whom he hath appointed heir of all things, by whom also he made the worlds."

Repentance (Gr. metanoia-metanoeo) means to have a change of mind or another mind [Matthew 21:28-32]. It also means to turn from sin and its ways, all disobedience, or rebellion against a Holy God [Matthew 4:17, 9:13, Luke 5:32, 13:3-5]. The power of repentance is phenomenal. **It is to change your mind to the mind of Christ** [Philippians 2:5]. It is to be godly sorrowful [2 Corinthians 7:8-11] for the sins that you have committed. Having a change of heart, we can now bring forth fruit that can speak without words, saying I am a changed man in my daily life according to God's Word.

Scripture Repentance

This kind of repentance is to acknowledge that the whole Bible is right. Whatever changes are to be made; it is to be made in one's life. The Scripture need not change. We must change according to the Scriptures. Why? Thus, <u>Jesus was born, according to the Scriptures</u>, He <u>lived</u>, <u>died</u>, and was <u>raised again,</u> according to the Holy Scriptures.

[Psalm 40:7] says, "Then said I, Lo, I come in the volume of the Book it is written of me." [Luke 24:44; Isaiah 7:14]

[Romans 3:3-4] says, "**For what if some did not believe?** Shall their unbelief make the faith of God without effect? God forbid yea, let God be true, but every man be a liar; as it is written, that thou mightiest be justified in thy sayings, and mightiest overcome when thou are judged."

We are to conform to the Holy Scripture in every phase of life, and not to rebel or resist any Scripture that is written in God's Word or be made a liar [Romans 12:2].

The apostle James said, "Receive ye the engrafted Word of God, which is able to save your souls."

Emotional Repentance

Repentance can be emotional. You must have a genuine change of feeling toward the sins committed. This change must be effective and operative in your life until you no longer commit that particular sin again.

[2 Corinthians 7:9] says, "Now I rejoice, not that you were made sorry with a letter, but that ye sorrowed to repentance: for ye were made sorry after a godly manner, that ye might receive damage by us in nothing."

[2 Corinthians 7: 10] says, "For godly sorrow worketh repentance to salvation not to be repented of; but the sorrow of the world worketh death."

Sorrow is a path that discovers self, distress caused by loss, affliction, disappointment, sadness, regret, grief, misery, and woe. Sorrow may affect one spiritually when man disobeys God. Through obedience, the blessings of the Lord maketh rich and addeth no sorrow [Proverbs 10:22].

[Psalm 18:34] says, "The Lord is nigh unto them of a broken heart and saveth such as be of a contrite spirit."

The Repentance of the "Will"

The change of one's will is one of the most important changes to be made. Our life change, when our will change. A changed will brings abought different results. A change of direction will take you down a different path. When God created man, he allowed the man to make a choice to serve Him or not to serve him. **Man is a free agent in the Earth. He possesses the power of his own will. Neither can God or the Devil violate his power of choice.** [Joshua 24: 22] says, "Choose ye this day whom ye will serve." This kind of repentance is an inward turning of the will in the man. This is when he gives his will over to God.

Let's look at an example of this in the Son of God:

[Matthew 26:36] says, "Then cometh Jesus with them unto a place called Gethsemane, and saith unto the disciples, sit ye here, while I go and pray yonder."

[Matthew 26:37] says, "And he took with him Peter and the two sons of Zebedee and began to be sorrowful and very heavy."

[Matthew 26:38] says, "Then he saith he unto them, My soul is exceeding sorrowful, even unto death; tarry ye here, and watch with me."

[Matthew 26:39] says, "And he went a little farther, and fell on his face, and prayed, saying, My Father, if it be possible, let this cup pass from me; nevertheless, not as I will, but as thou wilt."

Here we see that Christ turned his will over to God. This wasn't something he wanted to do, but He willingly gave up His will so that the will of God may be performed in His life. He gave up His will to the one who made Heaven and Earth. My way is not like your way, my thoughts are not like your thoughts [Isaiah 55:8], nor are my will like your will.

This is one of the reasons why some do not receive the HOLY GHOST with the evidence of speaking in tongues. They simply have not repented toward God. Although, it is possible to repent just enough to change ethically and morally, but not spiritually. For example, if you repent for smoking cigarettes, but still drink wine or beer, this is **not** considered true repentance. In order for true repentance to work, one must be godly sorrowful of all his sins and God will have mercy and forgive them for their sins. There's an old saying, **"You can fool some people some of the time, but you can't fool God none of the time."**

[Acts 15:8] says, "And God which knoweth the hearts, bare them, witness, giving them the HOLY GHOST, even as he did us. (The same as the day of Pentecost; [Acts 2:1-4] notes the time is A. D. 33 but this Scripture is A. D. 46)

[Acts 15:9] says, "And put no difference between us and them, purifying their hearts by faith." There is a purifying of the heart and only God knows the heart.

[Jeremiah 17:9-10] says, "The heart is deceitful above all things, and desperately wicked who can know it (you don't know yourself). I the Lord search the heart, I try the reins, even to give every man according to his ways, and according to the fruit of his doings."

But God prophesied to the people of Israel in the book of [Ezekiel 36:26], "A new heart also will I give you, and a new spirit will I put within you: and I take away the stony heart out of your flesh, and I will give you a heart of flesh."

The Way to Repentance

The part of a man that repents as a whole is the soul of man, which is made up of the intellect, emotion, and will. Only the engrafted Word of God is able to save the soul [James 1:21]. Repentance is a gift from God to man, and if one repents it is a blessing. The angels rejoice over one sinner who repents to God, but there are certain things that bring repentance. Jesus taught that miracles do not make one repent [Matthew 11:20] nor does one who has risen from the dead cause one to repent.

Only the Word of God and the preaching of the Gospel brings repentance. Acknowledging the truth and obeying its voice, can also bring true repentance unto deliverance. Repentance can be brought on through the chastisement of the Lord. The belief in the truth, and by seeing God for who He is, by vision or dream, and by the written Word of God.

[Hebrews 5:7-8] says, "Who in the days of his flesh, when he had offered up prayers and supplications with strong crying and tears unto him that was able to save him from death, and was heard in that he feared; though he was a Son, yet **learned obedience by the things which he suffered**."

There are many like me, who have been hard-headed and had to suffer extreme pain or catastrophe to wake up, repent and obey the Word of God.

The Prophet Jonah experienced catastrophe because he was found running from God. He didn't want to do the will of the Lord, therefore, he found himself in a world of trouble. He was on a ship with other people, that was about to be destroyed due to his disobedience. When he recognized the catastrophe, he told them to throw him overboard. It was at that time; he was swallowed up by a whale (which represents the world). The whale swallowed him up, he died and prayed to God. The Lord heard Jonah's prayer and had mercy on him. The whale spewed him out on dry land. After receiving mercy from God, the preacher had no more problem obeying the Master, the Lord Jesus Christ, and His Holy Word the Bible.

Sometimes, we have to go through trouble in order to come to Christ. We must be fully repented of our sins, in our heart, mind, will, and emotions, in order to receive the full effects of living life as a new creature [1 Corinthian 5:17].

Repent for the Kingdom of Heaven is at hand!

CHAPTER FIVE

The New Testament
WATER BAPTISM

Peter said unto them, Repent, and be baptized every one of you <u>in the name of Jesus Christ for the remission of sins</u>, and ye shall receive the gift of the Holy Ghost.
[Acts 2:38]

Christendom today has caused us to suffer the loss of good soldiers in Christ due to the lack of knowledge. [Hosea 4:6, Isaiah 5:13-14] The prophet Isaiah said, **"That the people went into captivity because they had no knowledge**, honorable men are famished, and their multitude dried up with thirst." He goes on to say, "Hell has enlarged itself without measure." This is because the devil has deceived a lot of people, namely Christians [Revelations 12:12; Matthew 24:4-5, 11, 24; 1Timothy 4:1-2].

The Devil knows the Scripture too. In fact, he quoted Scripture to Eve and Jesus. In the wilderness, he tried to tempt Jesus to sin by inaccurately quoting the word of God [Matthew 4:6]. As you read [Psalms 91:11-12], you will notice that he left out "in all they ways." No one is authorized to add to, nor take away from the authority established in the Word of God. [Deut. 4:2; Deut. 12:32].

We are not to tempt the Lord, but to obey His Word and He will keep and protect us [1 Samuel 15:22]. **The pretentious changing or forgery of Scripture can change your entire destiny by conforming to the alteration.** The devil is aware of this, so he cleverly uses one of his favorite methods; that is deception. As he makes attempts to clamber up the meaning of Scripture, he will get you to add to the Word or take away from it, consequently leading to disappointment. Furthermore, anyone who tampers with the Scripture would certainly suffer the consequences. This molestation to the Word of God occurred in the administration of water baptism.

<u>The changing of words and meanings of the Holy Bible is diabolic and a lower form of witchcraft.</u> At times it may be termed as written spells or automatic writing. What you read and believe, may become effective in you. **The power of words can affect your mind**. Remember the TV commercial, "You are what you eat, you are what you read."

Believers must be aware of the wiles of the Devil and be acquainted with God's Word. There are agents of the Devil who pervert (change its original meaning) the Word and most of them are false apostles, false prophets, teachers, and evangelist who misinterpret the Word of God. There can only be one Gospel, one God, one Lord, one Faith, and one Baptism [Galatians 1:8-9; 2 Peter 1:20; 16; Jude 1:3-4; Ephesians 4:4-6]. There are only two responses to the Scriptures, one is right, and one is wrong. There is no in-between, either you are cold or hot or you pass a test with an "A" or you fail it with an "F."

The Gospel records the life of Jesus and the Book of Acts records the life of the Apostles after Jesus Christ died, rose again, and ascended into heaven. The book of Acts is the life of Jesus Christ, working through his apostles to carry out His will. The Book of Acts is a book of action and loaded with facts. These facts prove to be true as they are released in the life of the believers. The book of Acts is the life of Jesus Christ, working through his apostles to carry out His will. Can any say that the Apostles disobeyed the Lord, or failed to baptize properly?

How Did the Early Church Water Baptize?

Let's take a look at the Scripture in the book of [Acts 2] after they received the HOLY GHOST [Acts 2:1-4]. The Apostle Peter preached that Jesus was both Lord and Christ [Acts 2:32-36]. After hearing such an anointed message, the Jewish men and the brethren asked the question "What shall we do?"

1. **The Place Jerusalem/ The time – A.D. 33 (The Church is born)**

[Acts 2:38] says, "Then Peter said unto them, Repent, and be baptized every one of you in the name of Jesus Christ for the remission of sins, and ye shall receive the gift of the HOLY GHOST."

Remission: n. to pardon; to forgive; release from debt, tax, etc.; to refrain from inflicting punishment.

So, we see that the Jews were baptized in the name of the Lord Jesus Christ, and not only that, there was a promise given in the next verse for future generations.

[Acts 2:39] says, "For the promise is unto you and your children, and to all that are afar off, even as many as the Lord our God shall call."

2. **The Place Samara/ The Time A.D. 34 –38 (5 to 6 years)**

The Deacon Evangelist Philip baptized the people of Samaria in the name of Jesus [Acts 6:5; Acts 8:5-25]. The Deacon Philip was trained by the apostles in baptism rites.

[Acts 8:12] says, "But when they believed Philip preaching the things concerning the kingdom of God, they were baptized, both men and women." [Acts 8:16]

<u>*All deacons that were taught by the apostles baptized in Jesus' name.*</u>

3. **The Place Damascus/ The time A.D. 35-39**

Saul of Tarsus was converted on the road to Damascus and became one of the last apostles, we have come to know as Apostle Paul.

[Acts 9:18-19; Acts 22:16]

[Acts 22:16] says, "And now why tarriest thou? Arise, and be baptized, and wash away thy sins, calling on the name of the Lord."

4. The Place Caesarea/ The time is A.D. 38-42 (10-12 years later)

At the home of Cornelius, a devout man, a God-fearing man, received the HOLY GHOST at the preaching of the Gospel by Apostle Peter. He responded by submitting to the Word of God and was baptized in the name of Jesus Christ.

[Acts 10:48] says, "And he commanded them to be baptized in the name of the Lord. Then prayed they him to tarry certain days."

5. The Place Ephesus/ The time A.D. 54 (21 years later)

The apostle Paul came upon certain disciples of John the Baptist and preached Jesus and the baptism in the name of Jesus. The twelve young men repented and were baptized in the name of the Lord Jesus Christ [Acts 19:1-6].

[Acts 19:5] says, "When they heard this, they were baptized in the name of Jesus."

6. The Place Corinth/ The time A.D. 59 (26-29 years later)

The apostle made it very clear that we are to be baptized in the name of Jesus Christ who died for us.

[1 Corinthians 1:13] says, "Is Christ divided? Was Paul crucified for you? Were ye baptized in the name of Paul." (Only Jesus name)

7. The Place Rome/ The time A.D. 60 (27-30 years later)

The Roman Christians were also baptized in the precious name of Jesus Christ according to the Apostle Paul.

[Romans 6:3] says, "Know ye not, that so many of us as were baptized into Jesus Christ were baptized into his death?"

8. The Place is Galatia/ The time A.D. 58 (29-32years later)

The Apostle Paul being in Galatia with the rest of the apostles verifies that the Galatians were baptized in the name of Jesus Christ.

[Galatians 3:27] says, "For as many of you as have been baptized into Christ have put on Christ."

As we see, the early church was only baptized in the name of Jesus Christ. Remember, we can't add to the word nor take away [Proverbs 30:6; Ecclesiastes 3:14; Revelations 22:14]. The devil knows how important baptism is, so he makes attempts to send confusion [1 Corinthians 14:33]. Those who fail to study the Scripture opens a door to be bamboozled [2 Tim 2:15]. The Bible wasn't completed for another hundred years after they started baptizing in Jesus' name. The New Testament hadn't been written or finalized. Even during and after this period and throughout the consummation of time, the order has not changed.

The Apostles had baptized in the name of Jesus for hundreds of years before the New Testament was completed.

They learned the baptism in Jesus' name under the law while Jesus was living [John 4:1-2]. Jesus instructed the disciples on how to baptize and they implemented it. Mary the mother of Jesus once stated to the disciples, whatsoever he says to you "Do it" [John 2:5].

What about Matt 28:19, is it not what Jesus said?

The Bible is the whole Word of God from Genesis to Revelation. The prophet Ezekiel said to eat the roll [Ezekiel 3:1-3]. God spoke to David and said, "Lo, I come in the volume of the Book." [Psalm 40:7; Luke 24:44]

[John 5:39] says, "Let's examine the Scripture for in them ye think ye have eternal life: and they are they which testify of me." [John18:19-21]

[Matt 28:19] says, "Go ye therefore, and teach all nations, baptizing them ***in the name of*** the Father, and of the Son, and of the Holy Ghost."

Father: n. (1) a male parent; (2) an ancestor; (3) an originator; (4) founder, inventor; (5) a priest; (6) a title.

Son: n. (1) a boy or man in his relationship to either or both parents; (2) a male descendant; (3) an angel of God whither good or evil.

Holy Ghost: n. (1) The Spirit of God; (2) The Holy Spirit (3) Note: a Spirit you cannot see! *Therefore, the impersonation is impossible.*

This Scripture above was commanded by Jesus Christ to baptize "in the name" not the titles "Father, Son, Holy Ghost."

Jesus said, I am come in my Father's name, and ye receive me not: [John 5:43]. Whatsoever you do in word or in deed do it in the name of Jesus [Colossians 3:17]. The name of Jesus is the Father's name.

Upon being instructed to be baptized, in the name of the Father, Son, and Holy Ghost, the question is "What is the Name?" And she shall bring forth a son, and thou shalt call his name Jesus [Matthew 1:21; Ephesians 3:15] of whom the whole family in heaven and earth is named. Behold, a virgin shall conceive, and bear a son, and shall call his name Immanuel, being interpreted God with us [Isaiah 7:14; Matthew 1:23]. The Son took on the Father's name. The name was concealed in the Old Testament but revealed in the New Testament. God sent a messenger; an angel (by the name of Gabriel) to deliver it personally [Luke 1:30-31]. God did not allow man to deliver that great name, that excellent name. You are a son or daughter and have taken on your dad's earthly name rather it be Smith, Jones, or Williams. You are entitled to that one name and not another man's name. When you are born again spiritually, you have a right to your Father's name "Jesus."

After working all week and you receive your paycheck if "Son" or "Daughter" is written on it, the check is not endorsed, it needs a name to validate it, to obtain and receive its worth.

Check is void there is no name

Check is validated there is a name

**Do you have your I.D.
Our I.D. is being born again**

Baptized in the "Name of Jesus"
Baptized in the "Holy Ghost"

The apostles obeyed the instructions of the Lord to the letter under the law and after his death, burial and resurrection they carried out his instructions under the law. John 4:1-2; Acts 1:2-3. Jesus opening their spiritual understanding, with the clarity they agreed to what He conveyed in His parables. Jesus used parables to hide certain truths from deceivers, false prophets, crooks and con-men [Mark 4:10-12]. The Father, Son, and the Holy Ghost are theophanies of God. Jesus the Word was the Father in creation (God in the Word) [John 1:1], the Son in Redemption (God in the flesh) [John 1:14], and the Holy Ghost in the Church (God is Spirit) [John 4:24], but this God has a name [Matt. 1:21; John 5:43; 10:30; 14:9-10].

[1 John 5:7] For there are three that bear record in heaven, the Father, the Word, and the Holy Ghost: and these three are one.

Therefore, since these three are one, these three have one NAME. You shall receive power after that the Holy Ghost has come. [Acts 1:8] Greater is he that is in you, than he that is in the world [1 John 4:4]. Jesus said it's expedient that I go away and if I go away, I will send another, for if I go not away, the Comforter will not come unto you; but if I depart, I will send him unto you [John 16:7]. When trouble comes who do you call on? We call on the name of JESUS.

[1 Timothy 6:1] says, "Let as many servants as are under the yoke count their own masters worthy of all honor, that the name of God and his doctrine be not blasphemed."

The name of God has been a controversy, ever since the days of Abraham, and even before that. Many religions and cults fight over what God's true name is today. The fact is, there are various names that describe God the Everlasting Father of Creation.

Each of the patriarchs and prophets saw God in a different light and used different names to describe how they saw Him. It was revealed to Moses that God will be known as I AM that I AM, Daniel saw Him as a stone cut without hands, which smote the image (The Beast). Ezekiel saw him as a wheel in the midst of a wheel. The prophet John the Baptist saw him as 'The Lamb of God," but out of all these names, there is only one name above all names [Philippians 2:9]. That is the name of Jesus Christ.

[Acts 4:12] says, "Neither is there salvation in any other; **for there is none other name under heaven given among men,** whereby we must be saved.

The apostles of Jesus Christ only used the saving name Jesus Christ when giving Him the glory [Acts 4:12]. My glory I will not give to another.

God will not share his name with another name, because there is no other name whereby, we must be saved. Every knee must bow, and every tongue must confess that Jesus is Lord to the Glory of the Father. The name of Jesus is the only name that heaven recognizes.

The Explanation of Matthew 28:19

* Notice the name is singular not the plural "One Name!"

* The word nations is plural not singular

* Father, Son, Holy Ghost are titles and not names

* The devil is a father [John 8:44].

* The devil is a son of God [Job 1:6-7].

* The spirit of the devil is an unholy spirit [Ephesians 2:2].

* Scripture never contradicts itself

* The name Jesus is the Family name in Heaven and on Earth [Ephesians 3:15].

* All works and deeds must be done in His name [Colossians 3:17]

* To deny His name is to operate in the spirit of the anti-Christ and spirit of error [1 John 2:22].

* There can only be One Gospel [Galatians 1:6].

* We are to speak the same thing and join together in the same mind [1 Corinthians 1:10]; be ye like-minded, having the same love, being of one accord, of one mind [Philippians 2:2].

Spiritual Laws

[Matthew 4:4] says, "It is written, that Man shall not live by bread alone, but by every word that proceeded out of the mouth (Bible) of God [Read Psalm 89:34-37]. When you open your Bible, you are opening up the mouth of God and He will begin to speak to you.

The law of Scripture states, "The Bible will interpret Scripture by itself;" it is to be put on par with the other Scriptures. Remember, there can only be one interpretation [2 Peter 1:20-21]. The law is very simple, the majority wins.

The Law of Moses "In the Mouth of Two or Three Witnesses" [Deuteronomy 17:6-7; Matthew 18:16, 19:15; 2 Corinthians 13:1; 1 Timothy 5:19], shall every word be established.

You must have witnesses to support your claim. One spectator wouldn't be sufficient [John 5:31-33]. If you don't want to die without mercy, try this case by the Law of Moses.

Even Jesus stayed within the confines of the Scripture, by not breaking the law but fulfilling them [Matt 5:17]. His words were confirmed by the witnesses in the Scripture, or it wouldn't be true. He said Himself, there must be a witness.

[John 8:14] says, "If I bear witness of myself, ye will say my witness is not true."

Even when God made "Man" the angels were present to witness, that it was God who made him and no other source. [Genesis 1:26].

The Witnesses in the Bible [Romans 10:15-16]

1. Apostle Peter

    a. Three thousand souls [Acts 2:41]

    b. Five thousand men [Acts 4:4]

2. Deacon\Evangelist Philip

    a. The people of Samaria [Acts 8:16]

      b. The Ethiopian [Acts 8:38]

3. Apostle Paul Baptizing in the Name of Jesus Christ

    a. The people of Ephesus
    b. The people of Rome
    c. The people of Galatians
    d. The people of Corinthians
    e. The people of Colossians
    f. The people of Philemon
    g. The people of Philippians
    h. The people of Thessalonians
    i. The seven churches of Revelations

Now, what I want you to do search the Scriptures and see if you can find just one soul being baptized using the three titles the Father, the Son, and the Holy Ghost? The answer is **- There are none!** They that have been baptized in the "Father, Son, and Holy Ghost" have failed to comply with the Scripture. The Scripture states be baptized in the "Name" of the Father, Son, and Holy Ghost.

[Hebrews 10:28] says, "He that despised Moses law died without mercy under two or three witnesses."

[Revelations 21:27] says, "And there shall in no wise enter into it anything that defileth, neither whatsoever worketh abomination, or maketh a lie: but they which are written in the Lambs book of Life."

NOTE:

THERE ARE NO BABY'S BEING BAPTIZED IN THE NEW TESTAMENT! YOU MUST MAKE YOUR OWN CHOICE TO SERVE GOD OR THE DEVIL. THERE ARE TWO DESTINATIONS BUT ONE CHOICE!

THERE ARE NO CHRISTIANS BEING SPRINKLED WITH WATER IN THE NEW TESTAMENT!

THERE ARE NO CHRISTIANS BEING BAPTIZED IN THE THREE TITLES: THE FATHER, AND OF THE SON, AND OF THE HOLY GHOST IN THE SCRIPTURE.

THERE IS NO MENTION OF A TRINITY OR DOCTRINE OF THE TRINITY.

Read the "Baptism History" Chapter (6), to find out where the Trinity Doctrine originated from and the trinity baptism. Its roots started in the Counsel of Nicea of the Catholic Church in 325AD.

The Bible mentions that there are seven Spirits of God, not three according to the book of Revelations. God is bigger than just three titles. He has seven distinct spirits [Isaiah 11:2; Rev. 4:5; 5:6]. Jesus said I am He who has the seven Spirits of God. We know from the Scripture that mention the seven spirits, that they are "held" by Jesus Christ.

THE BEREANS METHOD

[Acts 17:11] says, "These were noble than those in Thessalonica, in that they received the Word with all readiness of mind, and searched the Scripture daily, whether those things were so."

In the book of Acts, we find the Bereans were nobler in character and that they searched the Scripture for the truth of the matter. In order to do this one must use the Bible as the supreme authority. Let every man be a liar and let the Word of God be true.

Noble: to be morally good; superior in character or nature. A person of rank or noble birth.

Remember, they did not have the New Testament. They only had the Old Testament. So, there was Scripture that the Bereans either overlooked or didn't remember. They were convinced after Apostle Paul showed them what the Scripture said about the true Messiah.

The Lord himself agreed we ought to search the Scripture also to see if we have eternal life. This is done in a humble fashion. We must never underestimate the power of the devil. The believers can be fooled by satan, knowing this we must search the Scripture daily for any mistakes we might make or might have made.

[John 5:39] says, "Search the Scriptures; for in them ye think ye have eternal life, and they are they which testify of me."

Better safe than sorry!

Put your doctrine on trial!

Within thirty days Apostle Paul had given them all the doctrines of the New Testament using the Old Testament. The Bible says it took three Sabbath days to reason with them out of the Scripture. Wouldn't you like to have been in that Bible Class? Yessss!

CHAPTER SIX

Baptism History

The thing that hath been, it is that which shall be; and that which is done is that which shall be done: and there is no new thing under the sun. [Ecclesiastes 1:9]

King Solomon possessed an abundance of wisdom and because of this, he was able to apply it to various conditions in his time. He observed numerous trends come and go and concluded all is vanity and full of vexation. These things are even true in secular history. There is an old saying, "History repeats itself." I believe it is somewhat true because Jesus is returning back to the earth. Solomon once stated, "There is no new thing under the sun." History has the keys to the past and preserves a great reservoir of truth. Lawyers have the keys to legalism, and the saints have the keys to the kingdom of Heaven. <u>When they found the tomb of King Tut, they also realized and unfolded the truth of Moses,</u> and the same applies to the Dead Sea Scrolls, which mostly is mentioned in the book of Isaiah. History also testifies to the truth of Jesus Christ.

The history of the early church needs to be revealed to Christians. History concerning the early church has been in obscurity because what you don't know will not hurt you! Man has recorded history to ensure that their sons and daughters would learn and benefit from the mistakes of others. As parents, we know the world can be a cruel and deceptive dwelling place. To prevent the true essence of light from being revealed, various erroneous techniques are applied to upgrade deception applied to the truth. Therefore, as pioneers, as trailblazers, we make every attempt to protect and preserve history to avert our children from making prior mistakes and being deceived.

History is supposed to educate us, by shedding more light and giving us more insight into the truth. History sets the stage to deliver each child in its particular epoch from making an error and detrimental mistakes. Have you ever said to yourself, "If I would have only listened to my mother, I wouldn't be in this trouble! She tried to warn me, but I thought I knew it all."

THE EARLY CHURCH BAPTISM

[Acts 2:38] says, "Then Peter said unto them, Repent and be baptized every one of you in the name of Jesus Christ for the remission of sins, and ye shall receive the gift of the Holy Ghost."

If Biblical record is not enough to listen to, then give attention to the historical record.

A German Protestant Theologian "Gustav Adolf Deissmann" led studies on the Greek language in the New Testament. He said when the term name is used in this manner, (I baptize you in the name of) it signifies power and dominion. So to baptize in Jesus' name, we are placed in the possession of Jesus, we are at His absolute control.

Britannica Encyclopedia 11th Edition
Volume 3, page 365

Baptism was changed from the name of Jesus to the words Father, Son and Holy Ghost in the 2nd Century.

Canney Encyclopedia of Religion
Page 53

The early Church baptized in the name of the Lord Jesus until the 2nd century.

Hastings Encyclopedia of Religion,
Volume 2

Christian baptism was administered using the words "In the name of

Jesus Christ (page 377). Baptism was always in the name of Jesus (page 389).

Catholic Encyclopedia
Volume 2, page 263

Here you find the authorization acknowledged that the baptismal formula was changed by their church.

Schaff-Herzog Religious Encyclopedia
Volume 1, page 435

The New Testament only acknowledges the baptism in the name of Jesus.

Hastings Dictionary of Bible
Page 83

It must be acknowledged that the three-fold name of [Matthew 28:19] does not appear to have been used by the primitive Church; but rather in the name of Jesus, Jesus Christ or Lord Jesus.

[Acts 4:12] says, "Neither is there salvation in any other; for there is none other name under heaven given among men, whereby we must be saved."

Was there anybody trained of the apostles whom we do not know about?

Yes! They were called the *Apostolic Fathers*.

Their names are Clement, Hermas of Rome, Ignatius of Antioch, Polycarp of Smyrna, Barnabas of Alexandria, and Justin Martyr.

Clement of Rome - according to a Christian writer; he was consecrated by Apostle Peter. He was hypothetically identified with the Clement mentioned in [Philippians 4:3], which was taught of the apostles. He was a monotheist, a "One God" preacher, who was baptized in Jesus' name and a tongue-talker.

Hermas of Rome - a friend of Paul who baptized in the name of Jesus Christ [Romans 16:14].

Ignatius of Antioch - (67-110 A.D.) He was a "One God" preacher who baptized in the name of Jesus. He was killed by Emperor Nero after being arrested and thrown into a den of wild beast in Rome.

Polycarp of Smyrna – He was a monotheist, a "One God" preacher, who baptized in the name of Jesus. He was the last one of them mentioned, who was personally taught by the apostles (156 A.D.). He also was a martyr, which was burned at the stake and killed.

Justin Martyr - (100-166 A.D.) A philosopher who was scourged and beheaded in Rome with six other Christians. He was baptized in the name of Jesus Christ and filled with the Holy Ghost with the evidence of speaking in tongues. Baptism was always done in the name of Jesus until the time of Justin Martyr.

CHRONOLOGY OF SOME CHURCH FATHERS AND WRITINGS

The *Church Fathers* succeeded them and after them, the *Latin Fathers* emerged. By this time the Catholic Doctrine had changed and entered the flesh-absorbed, man-made doctrine of the Trinity created by a young writer; a lawyer named Tertullian who manufactured this deadly doctrine (A.D. 220). They plagiarized Plato's Timaeus (Plato took a triangle and geometry and put magic and religion together); in which it became the bases of the twisted "Trinitas" also known as the 'trinity'.

Here is the foundation of the Trinity doctrine in which the Catholic Church embraced, and many other religions emerged from this groundwork. With each proceeding generation, the people slowly drifted away from the original Apostle Doctrine, diluting the Word with their own propaganda. Through this prolific mechanism, many were misled by the Spirit of Error.

Polytheism- meaning many gods and goddesses more than one. These gods are not self-existence but rather fashioned from the substances God created or made. If God was created like these gods then there would be a greater power ruling over God. God is the self-existent God and is constant.

Trinity Doctrine- is a religious theory invented by Roman Catholic minds at the Council of Nicaea and completed at the Chalcedon Council of 451 A.D.

Catholic Bishops at Nicea abstracted God to be three Persons of co-eternal nature, but of the same substance. In the Latin Trinitas, meaning a state of being threefold. The theoretical unity of the Father, Son, and Holy Ghost as three manifestations in one Godhead, was imagined by the Catholics, as a union consisting of three in one. The word Trinity is not in the Bible. The God-head is not a person. Thus, the Doctrine of the Trinitarians can only be concluded to insert extra non-biblical or non-canonized revelation [1 Timothy 4:1]. Therefore, it is considered as a pseudo-revelation. "For in him (Jesus) dwelleth all the fullness (completeness) of the Godhead bodily" [Colossians 2:9].

[Deuteronomy 6:4] says, "Hear, O Israel the Lord thy God is one Lord." And we know that the Son of God (Jesus) is come, and hath given us an understanding, that we may know him that is true, and we are in him that is true, even in his Son Jesus Christ. This is the true God, and eternal life [1 John 5:20; John 1:1, 10:30].

GOD IN THE FLESH

[1 Timothy 3:16] says, "And without controversy great is the mystery of godliness; God was manifest in the flesh, justified in the spirit, seen of the angels, preached unto the Gentiles, believed on in the world, received up into glory."

The Bible only speaks of the people of Israel only having one God who is the Lord himself. God is like a champion, a heavyweight fighter, "He is the Heavy Weight Champion of all times!"

Whoever God is, he is the Lord; nobody but Jesus! [1 Kings 18:39; Psalm 118:27; Psalm 144:15]

[1Kings 18:39] says, "And when all the people saw it, they fell on their faces: they said, "The Lord he is God, the Lord, he is the God."

[Psalms 118:27] says, "God is the Lord, which hath shown us light; bind the sacrifice with cords, even unto the horns of the altar."

[Psalms 33:12] says, "Blessed is the nation whose God is the Lord and the people whom he hath chosen for his own inheritance."

[Psalms 144:15] says, "Happy is that people, that is in such a case; yea happy is that people, whose God is the Lord."

The Lord Jesus is declared also as the Word of God. Only the Word (Jesus) can reveal to you who Jesus really is! The Holy Ghost will reveal that they are one and the same.

[Matthew 11:27] says, "All things are delivered unto me of my father, and no man knoweth the Son, but the Father; neither knoweth any man the Father, save the Son and whomsoever the Son will reveal him."

English Form	**Hebrew Form**
God	El, Elah, or Elohim
LORD (All capitol)	JEHOVAH
Lord (Not capital)	Adon or Adonai

Looking at the English and Hebrew translations we see that all the meanings are attributed to God. Words are powerful and once released through the tongue can result in death or life.

During this time frame, there were others who held on to the teaching of the Apostles. They were known as the monotheistic Christians, Monarchians, Patripassians, Noetians, and the Sabelians.

They all rejected the Catholic idea concerning Godhead theology and rejected the Trinity as an unbiblical revelation. They held onto the Doctrine of the Apostles contending for the faith once delivered to the saints.

Pope Stephen a Catholic Pope declared the baptism in Jesus' name was the only valid baptism.

From Pope Zachariah we learned the Celtic Missionaries in the baptizing they omitted one or more in the trinity, **and so they anathematized them.**

Pope Nicholas (858-867 A.D.) in the Responsa ad Consulta Bulgarorum, allowed baptism to be valid in the name of nonime Christi, as in Acts.

Baptism *"into the death of Christ"* is often specified by the Armenian fathers as that which alone was essential.

Encyclopedia Britannica, Vol. 3, 11th Edition Pages 364-366

Urinus, an African monk also asserted that baptism into the name of Christ alone was valid.

In A.D. 34 when the Deacon\Evangelist Philip baptized the Ethiopian eunuch in the name of Jesus, they were both transported in the Spirit. Bishop Marvin Arnold gave a lecture at Midwest Bible College in 1994 giving us more information as to what happened to the Ethiopian eunuch.

In 1936 Bro. Charles C. Kirby was in Royal Oak, Michigan during a Sunday night revival with Elder Ross Paddock. Elder Paddock, the evangelist for the night was ministering when an elegant Ethiopian man walked in with his men. It was very peculiar, so they stopped the service to ask him who he was. He said, "I am baptized in Jesus' name and just wanted to come to church." This man was a prince in his country. He also stated that they were part of the church of the Ethiopian eunuch mentioned in the Bible.

In A.D. 37-42, history believes that Apostle Simon the Zealot took the [Acts 2:38] doctrine into England where they started the Celtic Apostolic Christianity. A thousand years passed, and history reveals that someone was building an apartment complex in Glastonbury England. While they were digging, they discovered the foundation of a church. It provided evidence of the [Acts 2:38] church. It was about 30ft wide and 70ft long. The archaeologist dates it back to apostolic times.

In A.D. 50-60, the Apostle Thomas indoctrinated Malabar India, with the Apostles [Acts 2:38] doctrine. The saints there were called the Saint Thomas Christians. He reached China also.

The religions of our time, have drifted far away from the original doctrine of Jesus Christ, which was handed down to the apostles. Somehow, new spectrums have risen and have adopted the Trinitarian Doctrine, without questioning where it came from. The Bible only teaches the Apostles Doctrine, which is Christ Doctrine, which is found in the New Testament [John 18:19-21; Hebrews 3:1; Acts 2:42].

These religions and denominations come from or out of the Catholic Church and made slight improvements, while somehow keeping the man-made Doctrine of the Trinity. If the apostles didn't teach it, and if it's not in the Bible, it's not True Worship!

Evil preachers crept into the church of God:

[Jude 1:4] says, "For there are certain men crept in unawares, who were before of old ordained to this condemnation, ungodly men, turning the grace of our God into Lord God, and our Lord Jesus Christ."

Hymenaeus, Alexander, Phygellus, Hermogenes, Demas, and Philtetus, left the true faith [2 Timothy 1:20; 2 Timothy 1:15; 2:17]. These preachers would not endure sound doctrine and wanted to contaminate and combine the Grecized-Latinized religion instead of holding to the Gospel in Jerusalem. They loved not the Truth.

In A.D. 66-90, they went out from us, because they were not of us [1 John 2:19; Jude 1-3]. Most were apostate Greeks who had been seethed into Platonism, polytheism, mythology, and philosophy. These men started their own religion and belief as opposed to the original message of Christ and His apostles.

[Philippians 4:8] says, "Finally, brethren whatsoever things are true, whatsoever things are honest, whatsoever things are just, whatsoever things are pure, whatsoever things are lovely whatsoever things are of good report; if there be any virtue, and if there be any praise, think on these things.

THE HISTORY OF THE 1900S

1901 - There was the famed Topeka, Kansas outpouring of the Holy Ghost. The glossolalia became well known in modern times.

1906 - 1909 - The Azusa Street Revival gained worldwide attention. People were filled with the Holy Ghost in California and according to history, the meeting lasted for three days and three nights!

1914 - April 15th, the Rev F.J. Ewart preached [Acts 2:38], near Los Angles, and conducted a tent revival. Glenn Cook and Rev. Ewart baptized each other according to [Acts 2:38].

1915 - The Rev. Frazee founded the PENTECOSTAL ASSEMBLIES OF THE WORLD. Around 1917 Bishop G.T Haywood became president of the organization.

1916 - The Assemblies of God rejected the [Acts 2:38].

1917 - On January 3rd, THE GENERAL ASSEMBLY OF THE APOSTOLIC ASSEMBLIES was founded.

1936 - At Christ Church Apostolic, in Royal Oak, Michigan, an Ethiopian prince who was baptized by Philip the Evangelist. This was affirmed that religion was current in his country.

1945 - In September, the Pentecostal Church incorporated, and the

Pentecostal Assemblies of Jesus Christ, merged and formed the United Pentecostals Church...UPC.

1948 – In May, Israel became a Nation!

1984 - In November, the Apostolic World Christian Fellowship Inc. had 8000 ministers and 55 organizations.

1986 - There is a powerful oneness Apostolic Organization in China, and Taiwan, under the name of the true church...... even in Mexico and Central and South America.[1]

---

[1] Inserts from the Apostolic Outline, Bishop Marvin Arnold

CHAPTER SEVEN

The Baptism of the Spirit

And they were all filled with the Holy Ghost and began to speak with other tongues, as the Spirit gave them utterance. [Acts 2:4]

The baptism of the Spirit is for everyone who desires Him, and for all who profess faith in Jesus Christ as Lord and Savior of their life. The first time the Holy Ghost was given to mankind was in Jerusalem. The Church of Jesus Christ according to [Matthew 16:18] was born on the day of Pentecost in the year of A.D. 33 [The Everlasting Church]. It was around nine o'clock in the morning, which is the third hour of the day when about 120 men and women were sitting in an upper room and a sound was heard suddenly as a mighty rushing wind [Acts 2:2]. It sat upon them like cloven tongues of fire. It looked like actual flames, but they were not on fire. It's a mirror of the burning bush. God was in the bush, but the bush wasn't consumed. Praise the Lord!

As we see in the above Scripture, "all were filled with the Holy Ghost" and it was about 120 people according to the Scripture who received it collectively at one time [Acts 1:15]. The Scripture says, "all spoke in tongues as the Spirit gave them [Church] utterance." <u>All waited for ten days to receive the promise.</u> Remember the word of God didn't say they had the ***gift of tongues***.

The Word Pentecost means "50th" and occurs fifty days after the Passover. In the Old Testament, it was referred to as Feast of Weeks, the Day of First Fruits, and the Feast of Harvests. It was celebrated on the sixth day of the month Sivan (our month of June).

The description of the Holy Ghost in the Holy Scripture [Acts 2:4; 10:46; 19:6] are a plumb line, a measuring tool, to test the spirit of professing religions and their diluted-doctrines. If it's not exactly 100% like the Bible, it reveals the error and exhibits a form of godliness [2 Timothy 3:5; 1 John 4:1].

[1 John 4:1] says, "Beloved, believe not every spirit, try the spirits whether they are of God: because many false prophets are gone out into the world."

Have you ever wondered about the number of churches on one block?

There are at least 15 different religions, organizations, and faiths on the same block, and they have the same Bible!

The Church is not just an institution, organization or club comprising good deeds. It is not a place of social entertainment. The Church is a living entity, an organism, and a sign of the proximity of the Kingdom of God.

Well someone has to be wrong. All cannot be right! If we go by the book; the Word of God will filter out all pretenders. For example: On your job or workplace there are rules and regulations that every employee must follow. **The rules don't change for anybody.** If the employer change, then he may be liable, and you have grounds for discrimination or respect of persons.

The Bible can be compared to our city traffic laws. If you go over the speed limit, no matter where you are, no matter who you are, the police officer has the right to ticket you with a violation. The traffic law is the traffic law, no matter what! To attempt to make an adjustment in the traffic law for your own personal convenience places one in violation of the law.

The traffic light is so simple nobody can misjudge what the colors mean; red means stop, yellow means proceed with caution, and green means go. There is only one interpretation for the traffic light without any adjustments. So, it is with the Holy Ghost; one way to receive it, with the evidence of speaking in tongues. There is absolutely no other way, as well as there is only one baptism [Ephesians 4:5] and no other way.

Find three people from each church and have them read a short story such as "The Three Little Bears" then ask them to interpret and tell what happened. Although each person may tell the story differently, each will have the same interpretation of the story. It's only one way. [1 Peter 1:20 it's only one way; John 10:1, 1 Corinthians 1:10].

[2 Peter 1:20] says, "Knowing this first that no prophecy of the scripture is of **any private interpretation**."

[1 Corinthians 1:10] says, "Now, I beseech you, brethren, by the name of our Lord Jesus Christ, **that ye all speak the same thing**, and that there be **no divisions among you**; but that ye be perfectly joined together **in the same mind and in the same name**.

THE SPIRIT FORMED THE CHURCH

The Church is not formed by man. The presence of the Church began by the Spirit, through the baptizing of all believers into the body of Christ. Therefore, we do not join the Church, we are born into the Church. This is alluding to prophecy of John the Baptist [Matthew 3:11] which says, "He shall baptize you with the Holy Ghost and with Fire!" John stated, "Except a man be born of the water and of the Spirit he cannot see the Kingdom of God" [John 3:3]. Therefore, there are two baptisms that are essential to be born into the family of God. Both requirements consist of one baptism and one Spirit. There is one body (one Church), and one Spirit, even as ye are called in one hope of your calling; One Lord, one faith, one baptism, One God and Father of all, who is above all, and through all, and in you all [Ephesians 4:4-6]

The Church is a spiritual building, a Temple, accompanied by spiritual power through means of prayer, fasting, and meditation on the Word of God. The Church should be built on Scripture, line upon line, precept upon precept, in other words, by the Scripture only. Our Savoir was born according to the Holy Scripture and died according to the Scripture. He also was raised from the dead, according to the Holy Scripture. Therefore, the Church should be built and operated, according to the Holy Scripture. Except the Lord build the house, they labor in vain that build it… [Psalms 127:1]. How strong is your house (Church)? A house has a foundation and is built with bricks. Each brick is held together with cement. Our spiritual house, the foundation, is Jesus Christ and each Scripture is considered a brick and the cement that holds the house (Church) together is love.

[1 Corinthians 12:13] says, "For by One Spirit are we all baptized into the One Body, whether we be Jews or Gentiles, whether we be bond or free; and have been all made to drink into One Spirit."

When God created Adam, He formed him from the dust of the ground and breathed the breath of Life (the Spirit of God) into him and man became a living soul. The same thing occurs in the birth of a child, and the birth of the Church. You are the Church once you are born again.

In the natural during pregnancy (first birth), your baby is surrounded and cushioned by a fluid known as amniotic fluid. This fluid-filled (water) membranous sac is called the amniotic sac. Within the membranous sac resides the baby and fluid (water). It apprises one that birthing will soon take place. The first breath of life (spirit), typically occurs within 40 seconds of the umbilical cord being excised. The baby no longer depends on the mother's nourishment and oxygen to enter through the umbilical cord. The baby becomes completely separated from the mother's umbilical cord. Upon the excising of the cord, it now separates the infant's will as an individual from the mother's will as an individual.

Being born again spiritually (second birth), a person is immersed in water (baptism). This person now becomes surrounded and covered by water to rise to walk in the newness of life [Rom. 6:40]. The name of Jesus is distinctly pronounced over you as you are immersed in water. The name serves as a mantle of protection and identifies you as a marked child of God. After baptism, a person must now receive the baptism in the Spirit, the life and power of God dwelling within a child's soul [Acts 1:8]. The first breath of this new life is when a child of God becomes endowed with power from on high [Luke 24:49]. It occurs when the child of God is completely separated from the power of sin. The evidence of this power is when a child of God begins to speak with cloven tongues of fire as on the Day of Pentecost [Acts 2:3]. This new life and power equip you now to live a holy and sanctified life.

Now in the natural, the child is a complete human being [Spirit, soul, and body], eventually, growth and development will take place. A baby is innocent and knows no sin. But because of the sin of Adam, the original composition is changed to body, soul, and Spirit, because man literally went backward. Due to Adam's disobedience, we are spiritual upside down and evil takes over us because we are born into sin [Psalms 51:5; Ephesians 2: 1-2]; the nature of the devil begins to work in the flesh [Galatians 5:17-21].

This is why our spirit has to be rebirth so that we can please God. Being born again is to have God breathe in us His Spirit and power to live above the power of sin! This will happen through the Spirit baptism. This baptism is a baptism performed only by God. Once baptized with this baptism, you become disengaged and separated from the world.

ONE BAPTISM WITH TWO PARTS

The bible tells the story of a man coming to Jesus to find out what it took to gain eternal life. Jesus told him that he had to be born again. Jesus explained to Nicodemus that being born again consists of two prerequisites; by water and by the spirit. The truth of the matter is there is one right way to be born in the water or baptized in the water. To be born of the Spirit is the second part of being born again. There is one Spirit which is God's Spirit, and not the breath of life which means you are born in the natural, this is a spiritual birth.

[John 3:5] says, "Jesus answered, Verily, verily, I say unto thee, except a man be born of the water and the Spirit, he cannot enter into the kingdom of God."

Since everybody is born the same way in the world everyone is born the same way in the Spirit. There is only One God, One Word, One Bible, One Interpretation, which interprets One Way, One Truth, One Life, One Father, One Son, and One Spirit which is Jesus Christ.

THE INITIAL OUTWARD SIGN OR THE EVIDENCE

There is an initial sign of a person being born in the Spirit, and it is speaking in other tongues. When a baby is born in the natural you know the breath of life has entered its nostrils when you hear them crying.

[1Corinthians 14:22] says, "Tongues, then are for a sign, not for believers but for unbelievers; prophecy, however, is for the believers, not for the unbelievers."

Speaking in tongues (Gr. glossals lalo) is considered by the Scripture as a God-given sign of the baptism of the Spirit [Acts 2:1-4; 10:45-47; 19:1-6]. This cannot be ignored!

Speaking in tongues is a manifestation of the Spirit. On the day the Church was born it was the Spirit who enabled them to speak in a language (Gk. glossa) they had never learned. Every nation under heaven was beneath them and heard and understood them because they were speaking in their own languages, and they had never learned their language. This means the Holy Spirit is very intelligent [Acts 2:5-11].

But why did God use speaking in tongues?

Well, let's go to the book of [James 3:1-18]. He tells us that a man can tame every kind of wild animal on earth simply because this is man's true birthright [Genesis 1:26].

[James 3:7] says, "For every kind of beasts, and of birds, and things in the sea is tamed, and hath been tamed of mankind."

But there is one member of the human body that has not been tamed by man; which is his tongue, and it takes God to tame his tongue, by the Spirit of God.

[James 3:8] says, "But the tongue no man can tame; it is an unruly evil, full of deadly poison."

In the Old Testament God showed his ability to control the tongue of a man. In the book of [Genesis 11:1-9], we see that the people of the earth were of one speech [Genesis 11:1] which represented the unity of all people. They decided to build a tower that would reach into heaven. This tower was called the Tower of Babel. The people created their own plan to reach heaven. The Scripture tells us it was God who came down and confused the language of their tongues to stop their plans because it wasn't time yet.

[Genesis 11:6] says, "And the Lord said, Behold, the people is one, and they have all one language; and this they begin to do; and now nothing will be restrained from them, which they have imagined to do."

[Genesis 11:7] says, "Go to, let us go down, and there confound their language, that they may not understand one another."

This same God that changed the people languages at the Tower of Babel, came surely in the New Testament to demonstrate His power on the day of Pentecost. He caused every nation under heaven to reassemble and hear the 120 to speak in their language by the Spirit of God. Upon this occurrence, being born of the Spirit, God gives us access through prayer to continue to build a Tower of Power that will reach heaven according to His blueprint. God was now ready for them to come to Jesus because the debt of sin had been fully paid for all mankind. Therefore, He sent the Spirit accompanied by a sign to all nations under heaven. Each of them heard as the 120 in the upper room experienced God re-establishing His control over man's Tongue!

[Acts 2:11] says, "Cretes and Arabians, we do hear them speak in our tongues the wonderful works of God."

This sign is also Old Testament prophecy: The prophet Joel foreseen this event. The Scripture says, "And it shall come to pass afterward, that I will pour out my Spirit upon all flesh; and your sons and your daughters shall prophesy, your old men shall dream dreams, your young men shall see visions; And also upon the servants and upon the handmaids in those days will I will I pour out my Spirit [Joel 2:28-29]."

Isaiah the prophet saw that the 'Spirit' would affect tongue: "For with stammering lips and another tongue will he speak to this people. To whom he said, this is the rest wherewith ye may cause the weary to rest; and this is the refreshing; yet they would not hear [Isaiah 28:10-12]."

Ezekiel discerned its effects on the heart: "And I will give them one heart, and I will put a new Spirit within you: and I will take the stony heart out of their flesh, and will give them a heart of flesh: That they may walk in my statutes, and keep mine ordinances, and they shall be my people, and I will be their God [Ezekiel 11:19-20]."

The Apostle John said that Jesus gave a sign that the Holy Ghost would speak Truth. The Spirit of Truth is infallible and inerrant. The foundation consists of Truth, the frame consists of Truth, and the fact is Truth. Pilate asked "What is Truth" Jesus responded by saying my "Word is Truth [John 17:17]."

[John 14:16] And I will pray to the Father, and he shall give you another Comforter, that he may abide with you forever.

When Jesus spoke of another Comforter, he was speaking of someone just like him. If I give you a dollar and you lost your dollar and you ask me for another dollar, but this time I give you four quarters. Well, the value is the same, but in a different form. One is made of paper, the other is made of silver, however, the same value. Jesus came in the flesh and the Spirit of Truth came as the Holy Ghost; however, they are one. I and my Father are one [John 10:30]

[John 15:26] says, "But when the Comforter is come, whom I will send unto you from the Father, even the Spirit of Truth, which proceeded from the Father, he shall testify of me."

[John 15:27] says, "And ye also shall bear witness, because ye have been with me from the beginning."

It is necessary to go in prayer for strength and to talk to God!

Prayer is a vital part of Christian life and a relationship with God. We must pray according to the Scripture, in obedience to our God, who inspired the Scripture. Here are a few Scriptures, which allude to the necessity of Christians having a prayer life, that adds to your artillery of spiritual warfare [2 Corinthians 10:3-6].

History references to the evidence of Speaking in Tongues

Schaff-Herzog Encyclopedia of Religious Knowledge
Vol. 3, page 2369

'Tongues, Gift of': A phenomenon of the Apostolic age, technically known as the 'glossolalia' of the Camisards, Prophets of the Cevennes, Early Quakers and Methodist, 'Lasare' in Sweden (1841-1843), converts in the Irish revival of 1859, and particularly in the Catholic Apostolic (Irvingite) Church.

Scaff-Herzog Encyclopedia of Religious Knowledge
Vol. 2, page 1119

'Irving, Edward:' 'In 1830 the news was spread abroad of the strange speaking with tongues which occurred in widely separated parts of Scotland. In 1831 prophecy and tongues appeared in Irving's church and Irving fell in with the movement, heartily convinced of its spiritual basis and divine authority.'

Scaff-Herzog Encyclopedia of Religious Knowledge
Vol. 1, page 422

'Catholic Apostolic Church': 'Pious Presbyterian men and women believed that their organs of speech were used by the Holy Spirit for the utterance of His thoughts and attentions.'

Encyclopedia Britannica, New Werner Edition
Vol. 4, page 749

'Camisards': 'Speaking in tongues, accompanied by all kinds of miracles, was common among the Camisards and Cevennes of Southern France in the 18th century. Children, under the influence of supernatural power, spoke and prophesied in languages unknown to them.

Encyclopedia of religion and Ethics, edited by James Hastings
Vol. 7, page 424

'In 1831 the gift of tongues and prophecy appeared. It was believed in answer to the fervent prayer, among the members of Irving's congregation.'

Butler, Christian Denominations of the World

'Edward Irving [1792-1834]:' 'He proclaimed his conviction that the gifts of the Holy Ghost, such as tongues, healing, ect., were withheld only because of the want of faith, and before long there were several persons in his church who claimed the gift of tongues.'

Abingdon Bible Commentary
Page 1190

'Scottish peasants spoke in tongues.'

Webster's New International Dictionary
2nd edition, page 1056

'Gift of Tongues': 'A phenomenon experienced by some of the Christians of the New Testament times. The nature of which seems to have a kind of ecstatic utterance usually unintelligible to the hearers and even to the speakers, therefore requiring interpretation; glossolalia. Similar phenomena have in modern times been experienced by some of the early Friends, Jansenists, Methodists, etc.'

{Taken from the Tract: The Apostles Doctrine 1567220975}

Prayer

Prayer is the breath that the spirit man breathes. For it was in prayer the Church was born and the Holy Ghost first came. The 120 in the upper room had been praying for ten days. Therefore, prayer is very essential to the new birth. After the new birth, God may use us in prayer to intercede for someone else or to pray for ourselves as we ought to pray.

[Romans 8:26] says, "Likewise the Spirit also helpeth our infirmities: for we know not what we should pray for as we ought (in the natural): but the Spirit itself maketh intercession for us with groanings which cannot be uttered. (speaking in the Spirit)."

Personal Prayer to God

This is a private line to Jesus' throne room, where one can send knee-mails to the King. Whatever position you find yourself in, you can tell Him all about it, without anyone knowing what you said, not even the devil. You are free to say how you feel. You can also worship Him, praise Him, and sing songs in which the Lord can understand.

For he that speaketh in an unknown tongue speaketh not to men, but to God (This is necessary!), for no man understandeth him; howbeit in the spirit, he speaketh mysteries [1 Corinthians 14:2].

For if I pray in an unknown tongue, my spirit prayeth, but my understanding is unfruitful [1Corinthians14:14].

YOUR SPIRIT CAN PRAY BY ITSELF!

Strength

Oftentimes, Christians are engaged in extreme temptations! It requires extra strength and power to cast out demons through fasting and prayer.

[Jude 1:20] says, "But ye, beloved, building up yourselves on your most holy faith, PRAYING IN THE HOLY GHOST (praying in tongues).

BEWARE OF FALSE SPEAKING IN TONGUES!

Speaking in tongues can be counterfeited by human initiative or demonic activity. There were churches in the city trying to teach the people in their congregation how to speak in tongues. Their members departed to receive the authentic Holy Ghost, which was encountered by the 120 in the upper room, as they spake as the Spirit gave them utterance [1 John 4:1].

FACTS ABOUT TONGUES

1. Speaking in tongues is an intelligent divine heavenly language that may be interpreted by God or them that have the gift of interpretation of tongues.

2. Speaking in tongues is spontaneous; not a learned phenomenon, nor can be taught by instructing believers to speak incoherent syllables.

3. The invasion of hypocrites; deceitful workers will disguise themselves as God servants [2 Corinthians 11:13-15]. These men and women will have satanic powers that seem to heal and even cast out devils, but these will be lying wonders [2 Thessalonians 2:9-12].

   NOTE: These workers are usually self-willed, self-reliance

full of pride and greed. They misinterpret the word of God very studiously. They count on you not to study or search out the original Scripture, written in the Aramaic, Greek and Hebrew language.

4. If anyone claims to speak in tongues, yet is not committed to Christ and the authority of Scripture, neither attempts to obey God's Word; or any other manifestation he or she may have, it may not be the Spirit of God [1John 3:6-10; 4:1-3; Matthew 24:11, 24; John 8:31; Galatians 1:9].

5. The genuine baptism of the Spirit will cause one to love God and man. Your fellowship will increase. When you love the saints, you will begin to abhor sin, and worldly ways. Your selfish ambitions for riches will dissipate and the Holy Ghost will give you the power to witness, pray, fast, meditate and read the Word of God.

THE SIGNS OF THE CHURCH OF THE LORD

The Lord has dispersed road signs for the wayfaring that are searching for eternal life. They that have lost their directions have accessibility to be redirected in the right way. If you ever went out of town there are signs all along the side of the road to assure you are going the right way, Jesus Christ is the Way for those who will follow directions and those who believe the whole Bible. Not some of it, but all of it. There are four signs that are constant: the Spirit is alive in a believer if all the signs are there in the Church you are on the right road. Remember, you cannot have one without the other it is a package deal. It would be like having Salvation without Jesus and we know that's impossible!

[Mark 16:17] says, "And these signs shall follow them (The Church) that believe; In my name shall cast out devils; they shall speak with new tongues."

[Mark 16:18] says, "They shall take up serpents; and if they drink any deadly thing, it shall not hurt them; they lay hands on the sick, and they shall recover.

THE SYMBOLS OF THE SPIRIT

Many times, in Scripture, we see God manifesting himself in things that can be seen with the human eye. The omnipresent God wanted man to see Him at God-given moments in their lives. In the days of Moses, He revealed Himself through a bush. It was something that could be seen by man and spoke from the bush in the way of fire. The ultimate manifestation was to be inside of a human body that He had created, to be seen of men, to be worshipped, to be crowned King of Kings, and Lord of Lords.

Here are some of the different manifestations of the Holy Spirit in the Scripture that alludes to the Spirit being poured out on the day of Pentecost.

    a. Oil [John 3:34]

    b. Water [John 7:38-39]

    c. Wind [Acts 2:2; John 3:8]

    d. Fire [Acts 2:3]

    e. A Dove [Matthew 3:16]

    f. A Seal [Ephesians 1:13; 4:30]

    g. An Earnest Pledge [Ephesians 1:14]

    h. Salt [Mark 9:49, 50; Matthew 5:13]

    I. Wine [Psalms 104:15; Ecclesiastes 10:19; Acts 2:13-15]

    J. Clothing [Judges 6:34; Luke 24:49; Isiah 61:10]

    K. Doorkeeper [John 10:3; 18:16-17; Psalms 84:10]

What is the Holy Spirit?

At that day ye shall know that I am in the Father, and ye in me, and I in you. [John 14:20]

The Holy Ghost is God in Christ coming to live in you [John 14:19-20]. It is the very personality of Jesus Christ. Everybody wants Jesus to take up residence, but Jesus wants to be president over your life, and to give you power over sin and to witness for His glory [Acts 1:8; to heal the sick and cast out demons [Mark 16:15-18, Isaiah 59:19]. The Spirit also guides and teaches each believer and brings "all things to remembrance, whatsoever Jesus has said in Scripture" [John 14:26; 15: 26-27; 16:13] the Spirit gives knowledge, and wisdom and understanding, and discernment between good and evil.

The Holy Ghost is also called the Comforter, which in the Greek (Gr. is Parakletos), "One called alongside to help the believer (The Advocate) to help the believer's shortcomings that he may be perfect in word and deed!"

The Holy Ghost comes to make men and women better fathers and mothers, better employees, better sons or daughters to our parents, a better neighbor to our community, and a better citizen to our state and country. This is what we call a new creature!

THE HOLY GHOST IS THE SPIRIT OF JESUS CHRIST:

- JESUS IS THE "FATHER" IN CREATION
- THE "SON" IN REDEMPTION
- THE "HOLY GHOST" IN THE CHURCH

The Holy Spirit comes to illuminate "The Inner Man!"

[Ephesians 3:16] says, "That he would grant you, according to the riches of his glory, to be strengthened with might by his Spirit in the Inner Man."

The inner man, the inward man, or hidden man are descriptive words that speak of the Spirit (1Peter 3:4). The inner man takes a seat in the soul which are the seats of feelings, emotions, and desires.

The Inner man consist of the soul and spirit, and its components "the heart," "the mind," and "the conscience" which make up the real you!

When God made man, He made him in His image. That image was both physical and spiritual. We were created to have the spirit of "love" such as our creator. Through the Holy Ghost, we are capable of giving pure love.

And hope maketh not ashamed!

"The love of God is shed abroad in our hearts by the Holy Ghost which is given unto us [Romans 5:5]."

THE FRUIT OF THE SPIRIT

In a dying world, people are not evaluating one's gifts, but they are fruit inspectors. They are examining our character looking for defects and blemishes. Our fruit determines how well we have submitted to God. The fruit is effective in our lives, as it assists in forming our character.

This is the lifeline of the "True Vine," much like the umbilical cord on the baby in the mother's womb. All of what the mother eats goes into the baby, and the baby begins to grow and develop into a healthy human being. The "fruit of the Spirit" is also to be directed by the Holy Ghost. By grace, these fruit help destroy the works of the flesh as we humbly submit to God and resist the devil. Grace refuses to work if humility is not present. If humility is not present the fruit will not yield an increase.

Three virtues that are within the Christian:

Love, Joy, and Peace are the disposition of soul.

Love (Gr. agape) is caring for and seeking the highest good of another person without motive or personal gain [Romans 5:5; 1

Corinthians 1:13; Ephesians 5:2; Colossians 3:14]

We link love to God because God is love. "By this shall all men know that ye are my disciples if ye have love one to another [John 13:34]. Love was the bond of Christian brotherhood in the earlier days of Christianity.

Charity begins at home. The church is made up of families. Therefore, we practice love at home, in the church taking it abroad to the world.

Joy (Gr. chara) is the feeling of gladness based on the love, grace, blessing, promise, and nearness of God that belongs to those who believe in Christ [Psalms 119:16; 2 Corinthians 6:10, 12:9; 1 Peter 1:8].

As an acrostic, joy has been described as **'J'** for Jesus and **'O'** for others, and **'Y'** for yourself!

Beware of sin! Worldliness can rob a saint of his joy, like parasites they suck the life out of a saint. If this is the case in your life, call on God as David did in [Psalms 51:12]. He said, "Restore the joy of my salvation." The prophet Nehemiah said, "Remember that the joy of the Lord is our strength [Nehemiah 8:10]."

The pleasures and treasures of the world are only momentarily. False joy can be compared to a smokescreen that masks your feelings and emotions temporarily. Only in the presence of God is the fullness of joy.

Peace (Gr. eirene) is resting in the quietness of heart and mind, based on the knowledge that all is well between the believer and their heavenly Father [Romans 15:33; Philippians 4:7; 1 Thessalonians 5:23; Hebrews 13:20]. Also, the state of response, harmony, order, and security in the midst of turmoil, strife, and temptations [Isaiah 45:7].

[Isaiah 56:19-21] says, "I create the fruit of the lips; Peace, peace to him that is far off, and to him that is near, saith the Lord; and I will heal him; But the wicked are like the troubled sea, when it cannot rest, whose waters cast up mire and dirt. There is no peace, saith, God, to the wicked."

THREE VIRTUES TOWARD MAN

Long-suffering, Gentleness, Goodness are the external manifestation in one's conduct.

Long-suffering (Gr. makrothumia) is endurance, patience, being slow to anger, or despair [Ephesians 4:2; 1Timothy 3:10; Hebrews 12:1]. This is putting up with others shortcomings, frailties, offenses, injuries, and provocations of others with the right attitude. Remember, you were in the same boat or even worse!

Long-suffering is love enduring because love is not easily provoked. It is patient while enduring injuries inflicted by others.

This is a quality of God himself, in that He put up with our faults until we repent and come into the perfect knowledge of God to a perfect man, just remember how patient God was with you!

Gentleness (Gr. chrestates) not wanting to hurt anyone or cause them pain [Ephesians 4:32; Colossians 3:12; 1 Peter 2:3] gentleness can be translated, "kindliness" or to be kind.

Gentleness is powerful. David wrote "Thy gentleness has made me great [Psalms 18:35].

A lot of times, we as saints harm each other because we lack gentleness with one another, causing each other pain and many tears in the night. Therefore, we must "be ye kind one to another" [Ephesians 4:32]. The Scripture says, "by lovingkindness have I drawn thee" [Jeremiah 31:3].

Goodness (Gk agathosune) is zeal for the truth and righteousness; a hatred for evil; it can be expressed in acts of kindness [Luke 7:37-50] and even in rebuking and correcting evil [Matthew 21:12-13].

Goodness is love in action. This kind of action is not all talk but doing the work. In the parable of the Good Samaritan, we see goodness working [Luke 10:30-37].

Goodness implies lightening the load of one who is suffering; a burden bearer, to suspend their load upon you by exercising goodness!

GOODNESS and GOD come from the same root word.

Goodness has power to win souls for God [Romans 2:4].

THREE VIRTUES DIRECTED TOWARD GOD

Faith, meekness, and temperance are the personal results in life and the character of the Spirit.

Faith (Gr. pistis) is a firm, and unswerving loyalty and adherence to a person to whom one is united by promise, commitment, trustworthiness, and honesty; a reliance on God in all He says [Matthew 23:23; Romans 3:3; 1Timothy 6:12; 2 Timothy 2:2, 4:7; Titus 2:10].

Meekness (Gk. prautes) is restraint coupled with strength and courage; it describes a person who can be angry when needed and humbly submissive when needed [2 Timothy 2:25; 1Peter 3:15]. The disposition to be gentle, kind, indulgent, even balanced in tempers and passions, and patient in the long-suffering without feeling a spirit of revenge. For meekness in Jesus compare [Matthew 11:29; Matthew 23; Mark 3:5].

Meekness is a grace of the soul that habitually submits to the dealings of God. Our attitude towards others has a lot to do with meekness within us, it can be said that meekness is ***Love with a bowed down head***.

There are many words that can describe meekness, but the foundation of meekness is realizing that we are nothing without God. This strange fruit has the power to forgive those who do us wrong.

Temperance (Gr. egkrateia) is having control, or mastery over one's own desires and passions and lusts, including faithfulness to one's marriage vows; also, purity, chastity [1 Corinthians 7:9; 9:25; Titus 1:8, 2:5]

Temperance is rightly handling one's soul, and to gain superiority over the carnal, by balancing one's desires.

Temperance is not just self-control, it is letting the word of God control your passions and desires, therefore being spirit controlled or led [1 Corinthians 9:27].

These characteristics must be practiced by the believer over and over until it becomes as natural as breathing.

THE GIFTS OF THE SPIRIT "POWER TO WITNESS

[Acts 1:8] But ye shall receive power, after that the Holy Ghost is come upon you: and ye shall be witnesses unto me both in Jerusalem, and in all Judea, and in Samaria, and unto the uttermost part of the earth.

The baptism of the Spirit gives the power to witness to the lost souls in the world today, with the manifestation of the power of Jesus Christ. He said, "Greater works than this, ye shall do because no man can come to God except God draw him." He told the prophet, Zechariah, "Not by power, not by might, but by my Spirit saith the Lord." [Zech. 4:6]

There are gifts that come with the Spirit. These gifts are for winning souls to the kingdom of God, for building up the church of God, and not for selfish glory; but so that the glory of God can be revealed to the sinner and to the world that heaven still has power! For in this present time you have false apostles and prophets, magicians, sorcery, witches, warlocks, and psychics using the devil powers to draw people to the devil.

THESE ARE THE GIFTS OF THE SPIRIT

The Word of Wisdom is a wise utterance spoken through the Spirit of God, to solve a specific problem or situation [Acts 6:10; 15:13-22].

The Word of Knowledge is an utterance inspired by the Holy Spirit that reveals knowledge about people, circumstances or biblical truth. This gift is closely related to prophecy [Acts 5:1-11, 10:47-48, 15:7-11; 1 Corinthians 14:24-25].

The Gift Of Tongues (Divers or different kinds of Tongues) is a manifestation of the Spirit, in an unknown language or languages, this is different from the speaking in tongues when you first receive the Holy Ghost, the Scripture says they all spake with tongues, not that they had the gift of tongues [Acts 2:1-4; 1Corinthians 12:10].

Speaking in tongues should be controlled or regulated in the congregation, the speaker or preacher should never be out of control [1 Corinthians 14:27-28].

Tongues in the congregation must be accompanied by a spirit of interpretation that communicates the content and meaning of the utterance to the community of believers [1 Corinthians 14:3, 27-28]. This is also equal to prophecy because the message may be a word of revelation, knowledge, prophecy, or teaching, for the Assembly [1 Corinthians14:6].

Interpretation of Tongues is a spirit-given ability to understand and communicate its meaning of the spoken utterance in tongues.

Prophecy is a special gift that enables a believer to bring a word or revelation directly from God under the impulse of the Spirit [1 Corinthians 14:24-25, 29-31]. Prophecy is not under the will of humans, but is directed from God and only occurs when God allows it.

Note: Prophecy is for the church. It is a sign to the believers that God is at work in the church or body of believers.

Discernment of spirits is the ability to distinguish between good and evil, prophecies, doctrine and/or utterances.

THE GIFTS THAT HAVE POWER
Faith, Gifts of Healing and Miracles

Faith is a supernatural gift, imparted by the Holy Spirit to enable the Christian believer to believe God for the extraordinary and miraculous works of God [Matthew 19:26]. It is FAITH THAT MOVES MOUNTAINS [1 Corinthians 13:2]. This is also equated or present with miracles and healing.

Gifts of Healing are given to the church to restore the physical and spiritual health by supernatural means [Matthew 4:23-25, 10:1; Acts 3:6-8, 4:30].

Note: The word (gifts) is plural which indicates that every act of healing is individual, unique and special. All members of the body possess the power to heal, but this power is above the norm.

Miraculous Powers (gift of miracles) are powers that alter the course of nature. God's divine power is demonstrated by his divine acts against satan and evil spirits.

THE PROMISE TO THE GENERATIONS TO COME

Apostle Peter preached the first spirit-filled message. Afterward, he uttered a prophecy to the generations to come that this would happen even to our kids and their sons and daughters until the rapture of the Church. Peter was also right in line with the prophets of old [Acts 2:37; Joel 2:28-29; Acts 2:17; John 14:18].

[Acts 2:39] says, "For the promise is unto you, and to your children, and to all that are afar off, even as many as the Lord our God shall call."

[John 14:18] says, "I will not leave you comfortless: I will come to you."

THE KEEPING POWER

[Ephesians 5:18] says, "And be not drunk with wine, wherein is excess; but be filled with the Spirit."

The Holy Spirit must be retained in the believer's life since he has two natures. Once he is born again, his life must be maintained by prayer, fasting, witnessing, and worshipping. With the Spirit presence and involvement, He leads one to a life of sanctification, and holiness unto the Lord.

[Romans 12:1-2] says, "I beseech you therefore, brethren, by the mercies of God, that ye present your bodies a living sacrifice, holy acceptable unto God, which is your reasonable service. And be not conformed to this world: but be ye transformed by the renewing of your mind, that ye may prove what is acceptable, and perfect will of God." ***Keep your spirit animated and flourishing in Jesus!***

CHAPTER EIGHT

The Aftermath of Being Filled

Then was Jesus led up of the Spirit into the wilderness to be tempted of the devil. [Matthew 4:1]

After being filled with the Holy Ghost, I was thrilled to learn I had received the genuine Spirit of the Lord God. As I returned home from church, I was confronted with the thing God had delivered me from; drugs. The dope man was at the door waiting and eager to get me high. For some reason, I thought my troubles were all over, but they had just begun.

[Luke 11:24] says, "When the unclean spirit is gone out of a man, he walketh through dry places, seeking rest; and finding none, he saith I will return unto my house whence I came out."

[Luke 11:25] says, "And when he, cometh, and find it swept and garnished."

[Luke 11:26] says, "Then goeth he, and taketh to him seven other spirits more wicked than himself, and they enter in, and the last state of that man is worse than the first."

After Jesus had been filled with the Holy Ghost, He was led into the wilderness to be tempted of the devil. It was there, the devil tried to get him to fall into sin, by using three major key weapons covered by deceit, and they are the Lust of the Flesh, the Lust of the Eye, and the Pride of Life.

THE BIG THREE

Lust of the Flesh [Strong's Gr. 1939 epithumia; Strong's Gr. 4559 sarkikos] it is a strong desire or craving of any kind. To delight in desires pertaining to the things of the world, as well as relating to its passions expressed in bodily activity. These devices are also known as the 17 works of the flesh found in [Galatians 5:17-21].

Lust of the Eyes [Strong's Gr. 1939 epithumia; Strong's Gr. 3788 ophthalmos] is to desire sinful things which will cause one to stumble. Moreover, the eye is the lamp of the body, and if your eye is not clear it will stimulate your appetite to the point you hunger for what is desired, no matter what it is. Here are some examples of devices that may be applied through passionate longing by the lust of the eyes: the desire for women or men, or perhaps both, covetousness, money, positions, and all things that will take precedent and allure you out of the will of God.

The Pride of Life [Strong's Gr. 212 Alazoneia] is vain boasting or vainglory; haughty; high-minded; showing oneself as being above others. It is demonstrated through self-righteousness, power, riches, beauty, glorying in oneself in sexual activity, titles and positions, and the pleasures and treasures of life.

[John 2:15-16] says, "Love not the world, neither the things that are in the world. If any man loves the world, the love of the father is not in him. For all that is in the world, the lust of the flesh, and the lust of the eyes, and the pride of life is not the father, but is of the world."

The world has a system of beliefs (Babylon); attitudes, desires, fashions, music, ambitions, goals, dreams, rules, and whatever society says is right. Beware of this spirit that comes to take you back into the world or make you look like the world, so that the world cannot see a difference between Christianity and the world.

<u>THE WORKS OF THE FLESH</u>

[Galatians 5:19 – 21] says, "Now the works of the flesh are manifest, which are these; adultery, fornication, uncleanness, lasciviousness; idolatry, witchcraft, hatred, variance, emulation's, wrath, strife, sedition's, heresies,; envying, murders, drunkenness, reveling, and such like: of the which I tell you before, as I have also told you in time past, that they which do such things shall not inherit the kingdom of God."

THE FIRST TEMPTATION

After Jesus was filled with the Spirit, He was driven into the wilderness to be tempted by the devil on all three major points of temptation. These are the same points that Adam and Eve were tempted on and failed into sin.

The first temptation was the lust of the flesh, the battle within a man's spirit that works against the flesh. It also describes the emotions of the soul, in which we have a natural tendency to indulge in sexual, carnal desires, and appetites. The lust of the flesh is anything that opposes the unity or harmony of the Scriptures, which regulate and discipline man's life. The Scripture is present to create balance in all things, rather it pertains to the flesh or Spirit.

[Matthew 3:3] says, "And when the tempter came to him he said if thou be the Son of God, command that these stones be made bread."

Jesus who had been fasting for forty days was famished for food. The devil was trying to make an offer to Jesus so that He may use the power of the Holy Ghost for His own selfish ambitions. It wasn't a part of God's will that He use His power for His personal gain. Jesus knew that His need was supplied by God.

[Matthew 3:4] says, "But he answered and said, it is written, Man can't live by bread alone, but by every word that proceedeth out of the mouth of God."

He is declaring that only by the Word will He rule and govern his whole life even what he eats and when he eats [Matthew 6:33]. Jesus was also showing us mastery over His body. The Spirit is to rule the flesh and not the flesh ruling the Spirit [Galatians 5:16]. The Spirit is the Head and the flesh is the tail.

THE SECOND TEMPTATION

Lust of the Eyes indicates looking at or longing for anything that is sinful; objects to desire, a fondness, for the glitter, glamour, glory, covetous, greed; a mental pleasure that is not of God.

[Matthew 6:22] says, "The light of the body is the eye; if therefore thine eye be single, thy whole body shall be full of light."

[Luke 4:5] says, "And the devil, taking him up into a high mountain, shewed unto him all the kingdoms of the world in a moment of time."

[Luke 4:6] say, "And the devil said unto him, all this power will I give thee, and the glory of them: for that is delivered unto me; and to whomsoever, I will I give it."

[Luke 4:7] says, "If thou, therefore, wilt worship me, all shall be thine."

The devil wanted worship. Self-worship is equivalent to worshipping the devil himself. Due to the fall of Adam, he sinned against God, corrupting his nature. The Apostle Paul said, "In the flesh dwells no good thing." In the devil lodges no good thing.

Note: I believe this is the ultimate disguise for the devil. Possessing many facets and various costumes, he is revealed through the works of the flesh. The Apostle Paul said, "When I would do good evil was always present [Romans 7:21]."

[Luke 4:8] says, "And Jesus answered and said unto him, get thee behind me, Satan: for it is written, thou shalt worship the Lord thy God, and him only thou serve."

Jesus forbade to open the door. What looks like an opportunity may not be one. Worshipping the Lord means to reverence Him, which consists in obedience to the written Word of God [Hebrews 10:6-9]. Obeying the written Word is the only weapon that can protect us under the covering of the Lord himself. Upon the application of obedience, it places one in a category of becoming a doer of the Word of God and not a hearer only [James 1:22].

THE THIRD TEMPTATION

In his third temptation, Satan uses Scripture to tempt Jesus. The craftiest lie told is mingled with the truth, to deceive the hearers, but if you hold on to the truth of Scripture you can't be fooled. This promise that is seen here is only for those who obey the Word of God. Also, we see the devil appealing to the pride of man to be somebody important; to know it all or to be recognized, honored and praised by proving to the world who you are or want to be.

[Matthew 4:5] says, "Then the devil taketh him up into the holy city, and setteth him on a pinnacle of the temple."

[Matthew 4:6] says, "And saith unto him, if thou be the Son of God, cast thyself down: for it is written. he shall give his angels charge concerning thee: and their hands they shall bear thee up, lest at any time thou dash thy foot against a stone."

The **Pride of Life** is an empty, boastful display of one's own resources; the desire for one's lifestyle to outshine his neighbors; a lover of possession of things.

Pride is rebellion against God; it was through sin that our first parents lost their original state of purity through pride. It is the beginning of all sin. Ignorance accompanies it and punishment awaits it [Genesis 3:5].

The pinnacle of the temple overlooked the courtyard so if Jesus would have cast himself off the pinnacle and landed unharmed, the people would have shouted that Jesus was the Messiah, but it seems that Jesus knew who He was!

[Psalms 91:11] says, "For he shall give his angels charge over there to keep thee in all thy ways."

Now compare [**Psalm 91:11**], with what the devil said in [**Matthew 4:6**]. The Devil left out *'all thy ways'*.

Jesus was also tempted on rightly dividing the Word of Truth [2

Timothy 2:15] and obedience to the Scripture [Psalms 91:11-12]. Satan only quoted part of the Scripture. Our duty is to obey all Scripture [Ecclesiastes 12:13-14]. Remember, one word can change the whole meaning of Scripture.

[Matthew 4:7] says, "Jesus said unto him, it is written again, thou shalt not tempt the Lord thy God."

The master key to victory is the Holy Scripture. The Lord Jesus Christ himself was born according to the Scripture, He lived, walked, talked, died, resurrected and ascended according to the Scripture.

[Colossians 3:17] says, "And whatsoever ye do in word or deed, do all in the name of Jesus [who is the Word], giving thanks to God and the Father by him."

The way to live in the Spirit is to be led by the Holy Ghost and by His written word in which Jesus quoted and followed Himself; so, obedience is the key to victory. The Bible is simply a book of rules to be obeyed, a road map to follow, which brings spiritual and natural victory and blessings.

[Proverbs 4:7] says, "Wisdom is the principal thing: therefore, get wisdom: and with all, therefore, get understanding."

[Proverbs 4:8] says, "Exalt her, and she shall promote thee: she shall bring thee to honor when thou dost embrace her."

[Proverbs 4:9] says, "She shall give to thine head an ornament of grace: a crown of glory shall she deliver to thee."

In the aftermath of being filled with the Holy Ghost, one must realize and understand that the devil hasn't given up on you. Just because you talk in tongues, as my pastor would say, he's waiting on you. The saint must sharpen his sword through much prayer, fasting, Bible study, memorizing Scripture, praising God, and attending church regularly to ensure that his or her soul is being fed.

The devil will use his tactics and schemes to entrap you in sin. The next phase is to destroy you in sin, as a tree falls, so shall it lay. If a person dies a sinner, he will rise a sinner.

The Devil comes to steal, kill, and destroy!

CHAPTER NINE

The Baptism of Suffering

But Jesus said unto them, ye know not what ye ask: can ye drink of the cup that I drink of? and be baptized with the baptism that I am baptized with?
Mark 10:38

In the above Scripture, we find that there is another baptism. The baptism of suffering. James and John the two sons of Zebedee, were seeking to sit by Jesus on the right and on the left side of power, and the question was asked, "Can you be baptized with the baptism that I am baptized with? [Mark 10:38]" This baptism was a baptism of suffering unto death. After the death, burial and resurrection of Jesus Christ, all believers confessing the name of Jesus, will suffer persecution. <u>They will be baptized with the baptism of suffering which leads to death for the Gospel and Christ sakes</u>.

[2 Timothy 3:12] says, "Yea, and all that will live godly shall suffer persecution."

[Matthew 5:10] says, "Blessed are they that are persecuted for righteous sake: for theirs is the kingdom of heaven."

Suffering can be described as chastening, affliction, trials, tests, and troubles. To undergo or to feel pain or distress, to undergo a penalty, and sustain the injury.

Since the fall of Adam, everyone born of a woman will suffer. Man, lives in a hostile environment, engulfed by both external and inner turmoil, and is "not at peace" with God and with self [Genesis 4:17, 19].

But suffering is something that the flesh doesn't want to do, and is contrary to man's will, so there is a rejection of suffering and man will lash out at the nearest person, and by doing so, will inflict more suffering.

[Hebrews 12:11] says, "Now no chastening for this present seemeth to be joyous but grievous."

The Holy Scripture states, after a personal encounter with God, two natures now reside within the believer. The old man and the new man who fight for control over the temple, which is your body. When suffering comes, the question is; who suffers the old man or the new man?

Only the old man suffers. Therefore, the old nature must be put under subjection, mortified, and removed [Luke 9:23; Acts 14:23; 2 Timothy 3:12; Psalms 34:19].

In the words of the late, Dr. Erick Buck, the 2nd Assistant Pastor of Christ Temple Church.

Why Must I Suffer?

The answer is the old man must suffer and must be continuously crucified daily. The flesh must be mortified. This is done to make room for the new man to develop and grow in the grace and knowledge of Jesus Christ. Which allows him to grow to maturity in holiness that can only be achieved through suffering.

The inner man is strengthened with might and power. As a Holy Ghost filled believer ponders on the fact that it is ONLY after and through suffering that this strength is acquired. Sooner or later great rejoicing will take place in the individuals thinking, which means we glory in tribulations.

[2 Corinthians 12:9] And he said unto me, My grace is sufficient for thee: for my strength is made perfect in weakness. Most gladly, therefore, will I rather glory in my infirmities, that the power of Christ may rest upon me.

Psalm 34:1 says, "I will bless the Lord at all times: his praise shall continually be in my mouth."

WE MUST ACCEPT SUFFERING AS THE WAY!!!

This basic suffering of Christians can be clearly seen in history and in modern-day times. However, how many times have you witnessed someone being ridiculed or faith tampered with because they don't want to do what others do, which is a sin? This is basically suffering because you're being talked about, lied on, ostracized and mistreated for the name of Jesus Christ. I am talking about giving up your life for Jesus Christ and being willing to die to self!

In some third world countries, you will die if you don't renounce your God and become a Muslim! To die for your Lord is to be a partaker of the baptism of suffering, as well as being persecuted for the name of Jesus.

In Egypt, young Christian women are raped by Muslim extremists and forced to fast and memorize parts of the Koran. In China, millions of Christians worship in fear. Many worship services are held in the homes of the saints. In China, the preachers are locked up and imprisoned, and even those who have a church in their home are at risk of being persecuted.

These are the countries to pray for where Christian persecution is most severe: Cuba, Libya, Nigeria, Egypt, Sudan, Saudi Arabia, Iran, Uzbekistan, Pakistan, China, Vietnam, North Korea, and Indonesia.

In American gangs on the east and west coast, the individual must be "jumped in" to be initiated into the gang. This is when the gang beats up the one who wants to join. It is like an evil way of baptism.

The Apostle Paul was baptized with this baptism at Lystra.

[Acts 14:19] says, "And there came thither certain Jews from Antioch and Iconium, who persuaded the people, and having stoned Paul, drew him out of the city, supposing he had been dead."

In another passage he accepts the highest degree, to die for the name of Jesus. Suffering through death is the highest degree as a person presents their body as a living sacrifice. Jesus' death was the highest degree of suffering as he bared the sins of many [1 Peter 2:24].

[Acts 21:13] says, "Then Paul answered, "What mean ye to weep and to break my heart? for I am ready not to be bound only, but also to die at Jerusalem for the name of Jesus."

The apostle James and John received the baptism of suffering Jesus said that they would in [Mark 10:39]. In [Acts 12:2], we see James dying for the name of the Lord Jesus Christ. John, we see on the Isle of Patmos, suffering for the name of Jesus Christ. They even tried to boil him to death, but it wasn't time. He had to write the book of Revelations. If God has something for you to do, you can't leave until it's finished.

Suffering brings about an exclusive anointing. This anointing consists of the baptismal of suffering. The Lord Jesus Christ could not die until His mission was finished and once finished, he stated "It is finished" [John 19:30]. Christ took on the baptism of suffering unto death, only to arise again with all power! Jesus' baptismal of suffering was over. His purpose was completed. The will of the Father was fulfilled in His life.

THEY ACCEPTED THE BAPTISM OF SUFFERING

Deacon Stephen: Died preaching in the name of Jesus. He fell into the hands of a religious mob that were self-righteous and they stoned him to death.

Apostle Mark: Was dragged through the streets of Alexandria.
Matthew: Perished by the edge of the sword.
Luke: Was hung on an Olive tree in Greece.
John: Was flogged first and then boiled in water and oil, and then placed on the Isle of Patmos to die.
Peter: Crucified upside down.

James: 1st martyred, beheaded in Jerusalem
Philip and Bartholomew: Were flogged alive.
Thomas: Pierced by a lance.
Mathias: He was numbered with the apostle; stoned and beheaded.
Paul: Was beheaded in Rome.
Jude: Was shot with arrows.

"THESE ARE THEY THAT LOVE NOT THEIR LIVES UNTO THE DEATH."

CHAPTER TEN

The Master Trick of the Devil

And the great dragon was cast out, that old serpent, called the Devil, and Satan, which deceiveth the whole world: he was cast out into the earth, and his angels were cast out with him. [Revelations 12:9]

One of the most powerful tools that the devil uses against us is deception. It was first used in the Garden of Eden and recycled in the Wilderness of Temptation. He uses this in the area of the Scripture, to confuse would-be followers of Jesus Christ. He is a master counterfeiter. He uses - false Christ's, apostles, prophets, evangelists, pastors and miracles to deceive onlookers and even a counterfeit gospel. If you take a counterfeit dollar it looks like the real thing when compared to a real dollar. When placed side by side, you can barely tell the difference. The differential is recognizable, due to its slight variations. Once the counterfeit is exposed, then it can be disposed of. The deception ceases, once God's power has been released.

So, line up your church with the original Doctrine as a plumb line and make void the traditions of men. Does your church line up with the teachings of the baptism of water and of Spirit? Do they teach that they are the same? Tell the truth is it the same? Variations of the Word depicts deception.

Deception: the act of deceiving; the fact or state of being deceived; to give a false impression that appears genuine; to lead astray whether by impression or influence;

Wiles of the Devil is not a temptation it is those clever schemes behind the temptation used to ensnare us through threat or intimidation. Most of the time the wiles of the Devil are never recognized to come from seducing spirits or the work of demons;

so, the spiritual war we fight is one of deceit and counterfeit.

Lies are false statements or false accusations with intentions to deceive.

The art of deception is to make something bad seem appealing. The famous magician Harry Houdini was a master at making the hand quicker than the eye. The Devil will often take his ministers and transform them into ministers of righteousness. He will even appear to you as an angel of light.

[2 Corinthians 11:13-15] says, "For such are false apostles, deceitful workers, transforming themselves into the apostles of Christ; And no marvel; for Satan himself is transformed into an angel of light; Therefore, it is no great thing if his ministers also be transformed as the ministers of righteousness; whose end shall be according to their works."

Deception starts in the mind and works its way into the heart. It is designed to trick you or to blind your mind, so you will not believe the truth [Acts 5:1-11]. There comes a time when you must pray, read, study, and meditate, on the Word of God for yourself.

[1 Timothy 4:1] says, "Now the Spirit speaketh expressly, that in the latter times some shall depart from the faith, giving heed to seducing spirits, and doctrines of the devils."

[2 Corinthians 4:3] says, "But if our Gospel be hid, it is hid to them that are lost."

[2 Corinthians 4:4] says, "In whom the god of this world hath blinded the minds of them which believe not, lest the light of the glorious Gospel of Christ who is the image of God, should shine unto them."

SELF-DECEPTION

One of the worst kinds of deception is self-deception. Many people tell lies and live lies to the point they start to believe their own lies. They have deceived their own selves. I heard a story some years ago, about a man who was a con-man that disguised himself playing different characters, conning people out of their money. His partner as well as himself were caught and went to jail.

The man was so caught up in his lies, he was still playing his con-man routine in prison just to get cigarettes. The con-man partner screamed at him and said, "Man we are not on the streets we are locked up, you don't have to play a con-game with me!"

We must confront our sins in life. We must be honest with ourselves. We must be true to ourselves. Our fleshly nature abhors being confronted by reality. Examining our lives meticulously will help one come to logic. Searching the Scripture will bring a person into true repentance and eternal life.

DENYING TRUTHS TO ONE'S SELF IS THE FIRST STEP TO SELF DECEPTION! DON'T WORRY ABOUT WHAT PEOPLE THINK OF YOU! SAVE YOURSELF!

[James 1:22] says, "But be ye doers of the Word, and not hears only, deceiving your own selves (this is the worst kind of deception)."

[2 Thessalonians 2:11] says, "And for this cause, God shall send them strong delusion, that they should believe a lie."

[2 Thessalonians 2:12] says, "That they might be damned who believe not the truth but had pleasure in unrighteousness."

- ✓ YOU MUST UNDERSTAND THAT THE BIBLE IS RIGHT AND SOMEBODY IS WRONG. IT IS THE FINAL AUTHORITY ON THE TRUTH, THE WORLD, AND THE DEVIL.

- ✓ FAILING TO BELIEVE WILL RESULT IN PAIN AND ETERNAL SUFFERING.

- ✓ STOP, LOOK, LISTEN AND SEE THE RED FLAGS BEFORE

YOU....! ACRONYM FOR STOP: STOP, THINK, OBEY, PROCEED

- ✓ **REPENT AND BELIEVE THE GOSPEL OF GOD.**

- ✓ **REPENT AND BELIEVE THE NAME OF JESUS CHRIST.**

- ✓ **REPENT AND OBEY EVERY WORD OF GOD.**

- ✓ **REPENT AND ASK GOD'S HELP IN OBEYING THE WORD OF GOD**

YOU CANNOT HAVE ONE WITHOUT THE OTHER!

God has revealed unto me, the master trick of the enemy that deals with three basic elements of being saved: water baptism [1 Peter 3:20-21], Spirit baptism [Acts 2:4], and Living Holy [Hebrews 12:14]. You can't be a partaker of one without being involved with the other.

1. If you are living holy and have not been baptized in the water you cannot see the kingdom of God [John 3:5]. Even if you are living holy and have the spirit baptism but have not been water baptized in Jesus' name you cannot see the kingdom of God. Cornelius was a good man but God required more of him [Acts 10]

2. If you have the correct water baptism in Jesus' name and living holy but do not have the Spirit baptism you cannot see the kingdom of God according to the Scripture [John 3:5]. This dual application of being born again of the water and Spirit must both be applied to your life.

3. If you have the correct water baptism and the correct Spirit baptism and not living Holy you cannot see the kingdom of God, according to [Hebrews 12:14] and [Galatians 5:17-21].

4. If you have the Spirit baptism and not the correct water baptism

and living holy you cannot see the kingdom of God according to [John 3:5] and [Matthew 5:19-20].

5. You must have all three to be saved and sanctified [John 3:5; Hebrews 12:4]. **This works like a combination lock; the lock won't open without all three combination numbers.**

The devil has set up counterfeit churches to confuse the believer. To find the true church would be like finding a needle in a haystack. God is not the author of confusion.

THE WORDS OF JUDE

[Jude 1:17-19] says, "But, beloved, remember ye the words which were spoken before of the apostles of our Lord Jesus Christ; How that they told you there should be mockers in the last time, who should walk after their own ungodly lusts. These be they who separate themselves, sensual, having not the Spirit."

Note: Remember the devil knows the Scripture and will try to use them to deceive you. He will also try to deceive you by not knowing the facts and qualifications of the different types of preachers. For example, if you don't know the difference between a false apostle and a true apostle, he can deceive you.

[John 5:39] says, "Search the scriptures; for in them ye think ye have eternal life: and they are they which testify of me."

The biblical rule of evidence is, "two witnesses" according to [John 8:17, Numbers 35:30 and Deuteronomy 17:6]. If I bear witness of myself ye will say my witness is not true [John 8:14].

THE DEVIL IS A LIAR

If the devil lied to Eve and Jesus, what do you think he will do to you?

Some of his famous words are:

- It doesn't take all that!
- You won't surely die!
- You know baptism won't save you!
- You know we all serve the same God!
- It's okay to do that, God is merciful!

But the truth of the matter is, there are two fathers: God and the devil. You are the children of God, which are the children of obedience; and the children of the devil, which are the children of disobedience.

THE DEVIL IS A FATHER

The bible says we are born in sin, so technically, we are born as the children of darkness, children of disobedience [Psalms 51:5; Ephesians 2:2]. We only become God's children when we are born again, and we speak as the Spirit (which is the Word, God, and Jesus) gives the utterance and we cry, ABBA FATHER IN THE SPIRIT.

[John 8:44] says, "Ye are of your father the devil, and the lust of your father ye will do. He was a murderer from the beginning, and abode not in the truth, because there is no truth in him when he speaketh a lie, he speaketh of his own, for he is a lie and the father of it."

Learn to resist the devil concerning his wiles, snares, tricks, and traps. Just like a salesman, he will try to sell you a lie! Make sure you read the fine print. Recognize smiling faces, and identify disguises, they are out there. They are close by.

One thing we must remember, in dealing with the devil God never took his power. He uses his power to deceive the people of God and the world. The devil has the power to heal, perform miracles, bless your finances, call fire out of heaven, send storms, affliction, and sickness, promote different religions, and will give you a church that belongs to him. Along with many other evil works and deeds, they are all designed to deceive and mislead you into sin.

[John 10:1] says, "Verily, verily, I say unto you, He that entereth not by the door (Jesus, the Word) into the sheepfold, but climbeth up some other way, the same is a thief and a robber."

[John 10:10] says, "The thief cometh not, but for to steal, and to kill, and to destroy; I am come that they might have it more abundantly."

The master trick is to get you to believe a lie, a denotation point of view instead of the whole truth of the bible and not just part of it. Be not deceived God is not mocked and He will have the last say. Even a true and faithful Christian can be deceived by the devil wiles and tricks, so stay under the mantle of the blood of Jesus, the one who defeated the Devil and led captivity captive.

For there shall arise false Christs, and false prophets, and shall shew great signs and wonders; insomuch that, if it were possible, *they shall deceive the very elect* [Matthew 24:24].

BE STRONG IN THE LORD

Finally, my brethren, be strong in the lord, and in the power of his might. [Ephesians 6:10]

In this Christian walk, it takes strength in God to make decisions of faith. After you have come into the full knowledge of the Word concerning baptism and living Holy, you will be held liable for following the right way. If the pastor is not following Scripture regarding these things, you must determine which direction you will follow.

The decision you make is based on your obedience or disobedience. Your decision will have effects on your eternal destination. If disobedience is present or any erroneous discussion involved, the Bible says that person is just as wicked! God is going to hold you accountable for your own judgments and decisions you make in your life.

[Proverbs 30:12] says, "If a ruler hearkens to lies, all his servants are wicked."

The Lord is saying the people who follow him are wicked too.

[Luke 6:39] says, "Can the blind lead the blind? Shall they not both fall into the ditch?"

The one following the blind is blind too. He won't be able to see the Scripture clearly.

TO BE STRONG YOU MUST
PRAY, FAST AND READ
YOUR BIBLE DAILY!

JUDE 1:20 - 25 (KJV)

[20] But ye, beloved, building up yourselves on your most holy faith, praying in the Holy Ghost,

[21] Keep yourselves in the love of God, looking for the mercy of our Lord Jesus Christ unto eternal life.

[22] And of some have compassion, making a difference:

[23] And others save with fear, pulling them out of the fire; hating even the garment spotted by the flesh.

[24] Now unto him, that is able to keep you from falling, and to present you faultless before the presence of his glory with exceeding joy,

[25] To the only wise God our Saviour, be glory and majesty, dominion and power, both now and ever. Amen.

CHAPTER ELEVEN

The Blood Test

Which were born, not of blood, nor the will of man, nor of the will of man, but of God. [John 1:13]

In the natural, we often hear of paternity sues of women taking their spouses or boyfriends to court to get a paternity test to determine the father of their child. In 1997, there was a young girl who accused actor Bill Cosby of being her real father. Bill Cosby wanted to do the right thing after admitting that he had an extramarital affair. Bill's lawyer's thought it would be a smart thing to take a blood test before going to court. To their surprise, he wasn't her father. The blood test proved that she was not who she appeared to be and was locked up in the penitentiary.

In Christendom, there is a paternity test to see if your Father is God or your father is the devil [John 8:44]. The best way to see which one is your real father, you must take the blood test!

An example of this would be through the story of Elijah and Elisha. When Elijah threw his mantle down to Elisha, the prophet ran to the Jordan River and cried, "Where is the God of Elijah?" The waters quickly divided as a witness that Elisha was now given the powerful Spirit of God that was with Elijah, before being taken away. He was the new prophet on the scene.

1 John 5:6 -12

⁶This is he that came by water and blood, *even* Jesus Christ; not by water only, but by water and blood. And it is the Spirit that beareth witness because the Spirit is truth.

⁷For there are three that bear record in heaven, the Father, the Word, and the Holy Ghost: and these three are one.

⁸And there are three that bear witness in earth, the Spirit, and the water, and the blood: and these three agree in one.

⁹If we receive the witness of men; the witness of God is greater: for this is the witness of God which he hath testified of his Son.

¹⁰He that believeth on the Son of God hath the witness in himself: he that believeth not God hath made him a liar; because he believeth not the record that God gave of his Son.

¹¹And this is the record, that God hath given to us eternal life, and this life is in his Son.

¹²He that hath the Son hath life, *and* **he that hath not the Son of God hath not life.**

The power and the life are in His blood, and the blood is in His name; because He purchased the church with His own blood. Therefore, we are in debt to Him and those who have His blood are obedient to His Word because He is our Father…Our dad!

HERE IS THE PATERNITY TEST

1. **Have you been properly baptized in the name of Jesus?**
   [Acts 2:38; 8:16; 10:48; 19:6; Matthew 28:19; Colossians 3:17]
2. **Have you received the Holy Ghost speaking in tongues?**
   [Acts 2:1-4, 10:42-48, 19:5-6]
3. **Are you living a separated life from the world?**
   [2 Corinthians 6:17-18; 1 Peter 1:14; 2:9; 1 John 2:15-17]
4. **Are you living a Holy life?**
   [1 Peter 1:15-16; Hebrews 12:14]
5. **Do you hate sin and the devil?**
   [Hebrews 1:9; Job 1:1]
6. **Do you love righteousness?**
   [Hebrews 1:9; 1 John 3:7]
7. **Do you believe that Jesus Christ is both Lord and God?**
   [John 20:28; Psalms 144:15; 1 Kings 18:39; Acts 2:36]

If you answered all the questions correctly Jesus is your Father. If for some reason you didn't answer them correctly, you have a spiritual blood infection and need a spiritual blood transfusion. If your blood is infected your heart is contaminated. A spiritual transfusion is required and may be obtained through confession, repentance, deliverance and constant obedience to whatever Scripture applies to the infected area. With much prayer and fasting, you will become a mighty man or woman of God in the mighty name of Jesus Christ saith the Lord thy God.

[James 1:22] says, "But be ye doers of the word, and not hearers only, deceiving your own selves.

CHAPTER TWELVE

The Eyes of Discernment

SATAN

Seeks his own will and wants sickness and disease.
He is not committed to the Word of God.
Lies interminably.
He has lots of churches.
Wants us to live in darkness and hide portions
of our life from others.
Wants us to doubt and disbelieve.
Works to make us disbelieve, or choose for
ourselves what to believe in.
Pushes us to disobey God.
Urges us to use God for selfish purposes.
Tells us our bodies belong to us.
Spares no effort to bring us sorrow and grief.
Desires our death.
Condemns and accuses us.
Pushes us to self-contempt.
Fosters discontent and grumbling.
Urges us to think we can get virtue in one big slug for life.
Urges us to concentrate on the sins of others.
Wants us to hang on to resentment and bitterness.
Urges us to have our fun now and try to
forget about paying for it later.
Tempts us to hide our sins and make excuses for them,
thus encouraging their feasting within.
Labors to believe temptation handled is sin.
Wants us to fail.

Encourages us in failure to wallow in
discouragement or despair.
Aims for us to wear a mask and act the part
by being all things to all people.
Seeks steady procrastination.
Strives to have us preoccupied with "what if".
Urges us toward a false, lofty super spirituality.
Labors to destroy all laws of God's and man.
Wants you only to see and obey some of scripture, but not all.

JESUS

Always obey the Father's will.
He is committed to the entire Word of God.
It is the truth!
He only has one true church.
Wants us to live in the light.
Longs for us to have faith in God's Word and to
be assured that He will always keep His Word.
Steadily assures us that Scripture is the Word of God.
Says, "If you love me, you will obey my commandment".
Longs for us to be used by God to help others.
Tells, us the body is the temple of the Holy Ghost.
Wants wholeness of the body, mind, and spirit.
Wants our joy.
Eagerly bestows life stretching on into eternity.
Assures us, "I came not to judge the world, but to save the world."
Assures us each man is infinite in worth to Him.
Urges contentment and praise in all situations.
Desires that we depend on Him minute by minute for what we
need and claim our "daily bread".
Tells us to look at the beam in our own eye and remove that first.
Tells us to forgive others in the same way God forgives us.
Influences us to pay now in time and effort,

then enjoyment is assured later.
Wants us to bring our sins to the light,
and have them forgiven, cleansed and forgotten.
Temptations are not sin.
To ask forgiveness, accept it, rise and go on.
Plants us a desire to be true to ourselves.
To let others know where we stand.
Teaches us now is the time of salvation.
Wants us to cultivate the present moment.
Wants us to depend on Him.
Desires peace, the fruit of righteousness.
Wants you to obey all of the Word.

SUMMARY

After the Ascension of Christ Jesus and since the day of Pentecost, water baptism has been administered specifically in the NAME OF JESUS CHRIST, for the remission of sins according to [Acts 2:38, 8:16, 19:5]; [Galatians 3:27] and [Romans 6:3]. The Scriptures agree and so does history.

The doctrine of the Trinity was manufactured by the Roman Catholic minds at the Council of Nicaea in A.D. 325 and completed in A.D. 451. The Trinitarian formula is the attempt to explain philosophically what Jesus stated in [Matthew 28:19] that could only be understood by revelation [Luke 10:21 -22]. It should be noted that the Apostles believed that Jesus was God [1 Timothy 3:16; Titus 2:10-13; 1 John 5:20; Jude 1:25]. The Father, Son, and the Holy Ghost are manifestations of God revealing Himself. Three manifestations, but one God.

At one point, the Catholic Church baptized in the name of Jesus but changed the baptism. One Catholic, Searle wrote, "If the minister baptized you in the three titles of the Father and of the Son, and of the Holy Ghost, he did not make you an Episcopalian, or Presbyterian, or whatever the name of your denomination he just made you a Catholic," says the Rev. George Searle.

All of these religions were not in existence when they changed baptism. When they started, they kept the Catholic baptism. The word Trinity is not in the Scripture, just like the word Pope is not in the Bible.

There is a broadway, and there is a narrow way. Frank Sinatra said he did it his way. Burger King said have it your way, but wouldn't you rather do it God's way!

[Pro. 12:15] The way of a fool is right in his own eyes: but he that hearkens unto counsel is wise.

BAPTIZED INTO THE BODY

WRITTEN BY BISHOP G.T. HAYWOOD COPYRIGHT 1914

HAVE YOU BEEN BAPTIZED INTO THE BODY?
BAPTIZED WITH THE HOLY GHOST;
THERE IS BUT ONE WAY TO ENTER IN IT,
JUST AS THEY DID AT PENTECOST.

CHORUS
ARE YOU IN THE CHURCH TRIUMPHANT?
ARE YOU IN THE SAVIOUR BRIDE?
COME AND BE BAPTIZE INTO THE BODY,
AND FOREVERMORE ABIDE.

2. THERE IS BUT ONE CHURCH, BRIDE OR BODY
AND INTO IT WE'RE ALL BAPTIZED
BY THE ONE, TRUE, PROMISED HOLY SPIRIT;
BY THE WORLD WE'RE ALL DESPISED.

THE CHORUS
2. EVERY CREED HAS CLAIMED TO BE THE BODY
BUT THE PLUMBLINE PROVED UNTRUE;
ALL THEIR DREAMS, FOR GOD, HAS SO DETERMINED
TO BRING HIS SON'S TRUE BRIDE TO VIEW.

THE CHORUS
3. MANY THOUGHT THEY WERE IN THE BODY
TILL THE HOLY GHOST HAD COME
WHEN THE WORD OF GOD WAS OPENED TO THEM.
THEY ENTERED IN,
AND YET THERE'S ROOM.

THE CHORUS
5. THOSE WHO DIED BEFORE THE HOLY SPIRIT,
CAME FROM ON HIGH,
MAY BY FAITH WITH SAINTS OF OLD DEPARTED
ARISE TO MEET HIM IN THE SKY.

THE CHORUS
6. WHEN THE BRIDEGROOM COMES, WILL YOU BE READY?
AND YOUR VESSEL ALL FILLED AND BRIGHT?
YOU WILL BE AMONG THE FOOLISH VIRGINS
IF YOU DO NOT WALK IN THE LIGHT!

ALTAR CALL

UPON THE COMPLETION
OF THIS BOOK, YOU POSSESS THE
POWER TO MAKE A DECISION.
I HUMBLY REQUEST THAT
YOU SUBMIT TO THE
BAPTISM IN JESUS NAME.

FIND THE CLOSEST APOSTOLIC CHURCH
NEAR YOU AND BE BAPTIZED IN JESUS
NAME.

BAPTISMAL FORMULA

MY DEAR BELOVED BROTHER/SISTER UPON THE CONFESSION OF YOUR FAITH, CONCERNING THE DEATH, BURIAL, AND RESURRECTION OF OUR LORD AND SAVIOR JESUS CHRIST AND THE CONFIDENCE THAT WE HAVE IN THE BLESSED WORD OF GOD, WE NOW BAPTIZE YOU IN THE NAME OF JESUS CHRIST FOR THE REMISSION OF SIN AND YOU SHALL RECEIVE THE GIFT OF THE HOLY GHOST IN JESUS NAME.
AMEN

THE WATER WAY

WRITTEN BY BISHOP G.T. HAYWOOD & HATTIE E. PRYER

LONG AGO THE MAIDS DREW WATER
IN THE EVENING TIME, THEY SAY
ONE DAY ISSAC SENT HIS SERVANT TO
STOP REBECCA ON HER WAY
MY MASTER SENT ME HERE TO TELL THEE
SEE THESE JEWELS RICH AND RARE;
WOULDN'T THOU NOT HIS LOVELY BRIDE BE
IN THAT COUNTRY OVER THERE?

CHORUS
IT SHALL BE LIGHT IN THE EVENING TIME;
THE PATH TO GLORY YOU WILL SURELY FIND
THROUGH THE WATER WAY;
IT IS THE LIGHT TODAY.
YOUNG AND OLD REPENT OF ALL YOUR SIN,
THEN THE HOLY GHOST WILL ENTER IN.
THE EVENING TIME HAS COME;
TIS A FACT THAT GOD AND CHRIST ARE ONE!

SO, GOD'S SERVANT COME TO TELL YOU
OF A BRIDEGROOM IN THE SKY,
LOOKING FOR A HOLY PEOPLE
TO BE HIS BRIDE SOON BY AND BY;
HE SENDS TO US REFRESHING WATER
IN THE WONDROUS LATTER DAY;
THEY WHO REALLY WILL BE RAPTURED
MUST GO THROUGH THE WATER WAY.

CHORUS
ARE YOU ON YOUR WAY TO RUIN?
CUMBERED WITH A LOAD OF CARE?
SEE THE QUICK WORK OF GOD IS DOING
THAT SO HIS GLORY YOU MAY SHARE
AT LAST THE FAITH HE ONCE DELIVERED

TO THE SAINTS, IS OURS TODAY
TO GET IN THE CHURCH TRIUMPHANT
YOU MUST GO THE WATER WAY

CHORUS
HAVE YOU OFTEN LOOKED AND WONDERED?
WHY THE POWER IS SLACK TODAY?
WILL YOU STAY IN THAT NUMBER?
AND GO ON THE MAN-MADE WAY?
O SAINTS WHO NEVER HAVE BEEN BURIED
IN THE BLESSED NAME OF GOD
LET THE TRUTH NOW SANCTIFY YOU
TIS THE WAY APOSTLES TROD.

THIS IS FROM THE NEW BRIDEGROOM BOOK S.N. HANCOCK
EDITION
PUBLISHED BY S.N. HANCOCK
CHRISTIAN EDUCATION INSTITUTION IN
LANSING, MICHIGAN 1106 N CEDAR STREET 48906-4419

CERTIFICATE OF BAPTISM

This Certifies

That _____

Date of Birth

_____

Place of Birth

_____

WAS BAPTIZED IN THE NAME OF JESUS FOR THE REMISSION OF SINS ACCORDING TO ACTS 2:38 THEN PETER SAID UNTO THEM, REPENT, AND BE BAPTIZED EVERY ONE OF YOU IN THE NAME OF JESUS CHRIST FOR THE REMISSION OF SINS, AND YE SHALL RECEIVE THE GIFT OF THE HOLY GHOST. [ACTS 2:38]

On the _____ day of _____ In the year of our Lord Two thousand and _____

In the Sanctuary of

_____

_____

Pastor

ABOUT THE AUTHOR

Terry W. Rogers was born and raised on the Westside of Chicago, Illinois. As a child, I was a victim of child abuse and began to sell recreational drugs at an early age, and as I grew older, I turned to the streets. I joined a street gang called "The Vice Lords." I began to go from High School to High School because of my gang activity.

Finally, I graduated from Holy Trinity High School in the year of 1983. In the year 1991, I became extremely addicted to crack cocaine, it was like Hell on earth without flames.

On November 17, 1991, I went home after smoking crack cocaine all night. I was supposed to pay my grandmother her rent money, but instead, I had smoked it all up on drugs. I was so distraught that I sought the Lord and He answered and said, "Go To Church." Shortly afterward, my grandmother came to collect her rent, I felt extremely despicable because I knew deep within that I had hurt her so badly. My grandmother quoted the same words that God had said, "Go to Church." That particular day she was going to church and I immediately rushed and put on my clothes and went to church at CHRIST TEMPLE CHURCH located at 14 S. Ashland Ave. There I was baptized in the name of Jesus Christ and I received the Holy Ghost with the evidence of speaking in Tongues!

After I received the Holy Ghost, I began to preach all over Chicago, Illinois. I began preaching and witnessing about the goodness of God, on the Chicago Transit Authority buses and Subway trains. As I preached, the power of God was "all over me and keeping me alive."

One day while preaching on the Ashland bus, the bus driver asked me to sit down or he was going to put me off the bus. I sat down and began to pray to God, "Lord I sure would like to have a job like this." Lo and behold about one year later I received two letters for a job offer, one was from the U.S. Post Office and one from the Chicago Transportation Office. It was a prayer that had been answered!

I began to drive the buses that I had once preached on so many various times and where so many people laughed and mocked me. I was now driving the CTA bus on the same route, with the same people, I once preached to. They no longer laughed or mocked me, "Praise the Lord!"

Later, I began going to the Cook County Jails where the late Mother Constella York ran a prison ministry. One Saturday in November 1992, there was a man preaching across from me at Division 1 in Chicago Prison System. This preacher turned out to be my REAL FATHER WHOM I HAD NEVER SEEN BEFORE! "Praise Our God!"

BIBLIOGRAPHY

Buck, E. (1981). *Illumination of the Inner Man*. Holiness in Print Productions

Buck, E. (1990). *Perfecting Gods People*.
Holiness in Print Productions

Search for Truth, Search for Truth Publications, Inc. 1981
Back To The Basics by Dr. D. Rayford Bell 1996, 1997

Salvation Guaranteed To The Sinning Saints? Copyright, 1987 by Dr. D. Rayford Bell.

Twelve Powers of Man by Charles Fillmore 1930 Unity Publications.

Something More By Catherine Marshall LeSourd CopyRight 1974, Mcgraw-Hill Book Co. Inc.

Apostolic History Outline, By Rev. Marvin Arnold, D.D., Th.D. Arno Publications United States Copyright March 1986

Ministerial Manual of Discipline of the Pentecostal Churches of the Apostolic Faith Inc.

Nicaea and The Council Of A.D.325 By Rev. Marvin M. Arnold, D.D., Th.D. Copyright 1987 Arno Publications.

All About The Holy Spirit By Hubert Lockyer, D.D. Zondervan Publishing House 1415, Lake Dr. S.E. Grand Rapids, Michigan 49506. CopyRights 1975

Lectures In Systematic Theology; By Hebry Clarence Thiessen, Revised By Vernin D. Dorerksen, William B. Eerdmans Publishing Company: Grand Rapids, Michigan.

STUDY BIBLES

The Full Life Study Bible New International Version Zondervan publishing house copy right 1973, 1978, 1984, 1992; pp 1770, 1642, 1646.

The Scofield Study Bible, New York University Press, copyright 1909, 1917; renewed 1945.

The Dakes Annotated Study Bible, copyright 1963 by 1991 by Finis Jennings Dake

REDEEM TEAM

HOME OF THE STREET PREACHERS

We are dedicated to informing you of the whole counsel of God's Word. This book is an exposition of the Truth on the subject of water baptism, Spirit baptism, the baptism of fire, and the baptism of death or martyrdom.

OTHER PUBLICATIONS
WRITTEN AND COMPILED
BY: BISHOP TERRY W. ROGERS SR.

* ARE THERE APOSTLES TODAY 12.00
* THE TRUTH ABOUT PROPHETS TODAY 12.00
* A TRUE EVANGELIST 12.00
* The CALL OF THE TEACHER 12.00
* The LORD'S PASTOR 12.00
* HOW TO TARRY FOR THE HOLY GHOST 2.00
* THE HOLY GHOST POSSE STREET MINISTRY 10.00

BOOKS BY BISHOP DR. D RAYFORD BELL

THE PRESIDING BISHOP OF THE P.C.A.F.
SALVATION GUARANTEED TO THE SINNING SAINTS? 5.00
MARRIAGES ARE NOT MADE IN HEAVEN 5:00
THE PHILOSOPHY OF CHRIST 7.00
BACK TO THE BASICS 10.00

BOOKS BY PROFESSOR ELDER ERIC BUCK
PERFECTING GODS PEOPLE 5.00

BOOKS BY EVANGELIST ALICE J. BONK
SPIRITUAL WARFARE ACTION TEAM MANUAL 5.00

PLEASE ADD $2.00 FOR SHIPPING COST

Make Checks Payable To

BISHOP TERRY W. ROGERS SR.

UPPER ROOM A.F.C.

PO BOX 1101

MONTGOMERY, IL 60538

Ministry Phone: 1(331)262-1627

SUPPORT THE APOSTOLIC STREET MINISTRY

SOWING SEED ON GOOD GROUND

CONTACT DATA

- Bishop Terry Rogers
  Cash.me/$BishopTerryRogers

- Upper Room Apostolic Faith Church
  Or Bishop Terry Rogers Sr.
  P.O. Box 1101
  Montgomery, Illinois 60538

- www.gofundme.com/upper-room-church
  Upper Room Apostolic Faith Church
  137 So. Pulaski Rd.
  Chicago, Illinois 60624
  Bishop Terry Rogers Sr.

The Redeem Team Home of the Street Preachers
We request that you consider investing in
Kingdom building by supporting
the Outreach Ministry and becoming a sponsor by
making monthly contributions of any size.
This is guaranteed good grounds to
sow upon, the dividends are great.
"The blessings of the Lord
it maketh rich and it adds no sorrow."
[Proverbs 10:22]

Also, the ministry may be followed on:

Facebook	@TerryRogers
	@WayneRogers
Twitter	@bishop22161
Periscope	@terryrogers101

Cloven Tongues of Fire
Prayer line
1(331)262-1627

Made in the USA
Lexington, KY
05 November 2019